EXPERIENCE & THEORY

Experience & Theory

\\\

Edited by Lawrence Foster & J. W. Swanson

 DUCKWORTH

First published in Great Britain by Gerald Duckworth &
Company Limited, 3 Henrietta Street, London, W.C.2.

© 1970 *University of Massachusetts Press*

This book was not designed in Great Britain but printed from
photographic plates of the American edition.

ISBN 0 7156 0603 4

Printed by Compton Printing Ltd.,
London and Aylesbury.

In Memoriam
J. W. Swanson (1926–1969)

Contents

Preface

IN THE ACADEMIC year 1968–1969 the University of Massachusetts at Amherst offered a faculty-student seminar on the topic "Experience and Theory." The papers included in this volume were originally presented at a public lecture series offered in conjunction with the seminar. In most cases the lectures have been slightly revised for publication.

What distinguishes experience from theory or the experiential from the theoretical? The answer is far from clear. Quine, in "Grades of Theoreticity," examines two problems: the nature of the data of experience and the differing grades of theoreticity or distances from this data. In the course of his investigation he provides an analysis of the technical notion of an observation sentence and also discusses the extent of ostensive learning. He concludes with some illuminating remarks on the theoretical level of the ideas of individuation and objectual quantification.

In the construction of theories to account for certain aspects of experience philosophers frequently appeal to the relation of similarity or resemblance. Traditionally, this relation has been assumed to be both clear and serviceable. Goodman, in "Seven Strictures on Similarity," investigates several areas where this relation has been employed in the solution of a philosophical problem. In each case Goodman argues that recourse to this relation is singularly unhelpful. His claim, if true, takes away "one more handy tool from the philosopher's dwindling kit," and undermines numerous theories in areas ranging from aesthetics to the philosophy of science.

The next three papers take as their point of departure Kant's *Critique of Pure Reason*. Perhaps this should not be surprising since a major portion of the *Critique* is concerned with how experience and theory come together to make empirical knowledge possible. In the most purely historical of the seven essays, Strawson, in "Imagination and Perception," focuses on Kant's treatment of the role of imagination as a necessary ingredient in perceptual recognition. Kant's analysis of what is involved in perceiving "an enduring object as an enduring object of a certain kind" is examined. In the course of this study Strawson sets forth Kant's views on the nature of the imagination and its function in perception, and then contrasts them with the views of Hume and the later Wittgenstein.

Like Strawson, Sellars, in "Toward a Theory of the Categories," contrasts the views of Kant and Wittgenstein, but it is the Wittgenstein of the *Tractatus* rather than of the *Philosophical Investigations* whom he considers. "Both Kant and Wittgenstein think it possible to give an a priori account of what it is to be an object of empirical knowledge." Sellars claims that the starting point for both philosophers was the structure of logical theory as known in their time. He contends that both Kant and Wittgenstein require a theory of categories in their explication of the concept of an object of empirical knowledge. The major portion of Sellars' essay is devoted to the development of such a theory.

The Kantian problem of reconciling freedom with causal determinism is the concern of Davidson's paper, "Mental Events." Mental events, such as perceivings, decisions, and actions, are admitted as playing a causal role in the physical world. Yet where there is causality there must be deterministic laws. But if this be true, how is freedom possible? Davidson proposes to reconcile freedom with causal determinism by arguing that although mental and physical events are causally related, the correlated deterministic laws cannot be psychophysical ones. He concludes by defending a version of the identity theory of mind and body.

Chisholm's task in "On the Nature of Empirical Evidence" is to give an account of certain fundamental epistemic concepts. On the basis of an undefined notion of epistemic preferability he first attempts to account for the chief concepts and principles pertaining to the epistemic status that a single proposition may have for a given subject at a given time. He then proceeds to define certain epistemic relations, such as *x inductively confers evidence upon y*, which may hold between two propositions. Next, he employs some of these resulting concepts and principles in an impressive attempt to define knowledge. In the final section Chisholm formulates criteria of application for a number of epistemic terms.

Developing principles of evidence is one task; justifying them is another. Where Chisholm concerns himself with the first problem, Black, in "Induction and Experience," deals with the second. He considers anew the age-old problem of justifying induction and attempts to show that inductive rules can be supported by an appeal to past experience. In his view such a justification does not fall prey to the charge of circularity and it does not force us to accept analogous support for counterinductive rules.

The editors wish to thank the Graduate School and the College of Arts and Sciences of the University of Massachusetts at Amherst for making the lecture series possible. They are especially grateful to Deans Edward C. Moore, Arthur C. Gentile, and I. Moyer Hunsberger, who were directly responsible for financing the series, and to Bruce Aune, Head of the Department of Philosophy, who conceived of the series and arranged its support. Leone Stein and Paul M. Wright of the University of Massachusetts Press are thanked for their help and cooperation in the preparation of this volume.

One of the editors, J. W. Swanson, did not live to see this book appear in print. He is dearly missed.

LAWRENCE FOSTER

W. V. Quine
Grades of Theoreticity

THE NOTION of a molecule or positron is more theoretical than
that of a golf ball or rabbit. By this I mean that it is more remote
from the data. The notion of a golf ball or rabbit is in turn more
theoretical, in my view, than the notion of water or rubber; but
this will take some explaining. I propose in this paper to examine some of the differences between one grade of theoreticity
and another.

Preparatory to assessing grades of theoreticity, or distances
from the data, we ought to settle what to count as data. They are
supposed to be, as nearly as possible, the uninterpreted testimony of the senses. Thus it was that Berkeley and others have
conceived of our visual data as two dimensional and looked upon
three-dimensional vision as the product of interpretation. The
primacy of two-dimensional vision is a matter of optics: man's
three-dimensional eye intercepts three-dimensional light along
a two-dimensional surface.

If a philosopher is as intent as Berkeley was on doubting the
physical world, there is irony in his basing his notion of sense
datum on optics. Introspection would seem to be more to the
point. Now introspection tells us that what we are first aware of
in vision are not two-dimensional patches of color, but three-
dimensional bodies. The color patches are products of abstrac-
tion. Some skill and sophistication are needed, even, in ab-
stracting them. Painters have to be trained to it.

Since data are supposed to be hard and incontestable, it is
ironical that the very notion of datum should be shaky and controversial. In the appeal to introspection there is a further irony;
introspection is a curiously soft basis on which to decide what to
count as hard data. I am amassing ironies; this makes three already. Still, psychological experiment can be cited instead of
introspection to show that physical objects or other structured
wholes are in some sense more fundamental than the sensory
bits and patches that can be abstracted out of them.

In the question what to count as data, thus, two forces strain against each other. Force 1 favors causal proximity to the physical stimulus. Force 2 favors the focus of awareness. Now the notion of datum has been under strain by these two forces only because of the traditional epistemological purpose which the notion of datum was to serve. Epistemologists dreamed of a first philosophy, firmer than science and serving to justify our knowledge of the external world. Certainly, if an epistemologist wants to explain how a man might rationally construct or project a theory of the external world from his sense data, he wants these data to be something a man can be aware of. Insofar, Force 2 asserts itself. Yet this same epistemologist is bound to take the world of bodies and physical stimulation seriously too in his way, since it is precisely our knowledge of this that he is so heroically trying to justify. It would be reassuring to him to find that his epistemological construction of the external world was recapitulated, to some degree, within the external world in the processes by which physical people form habits in response to physical stimulations. This would encourage him to feel that he had epistemologically constructed the right external world by the right steps. Force 1, then, the force for proximity of datum to physical stimulus, gets at him in this way, and hence the strain.

The dilemma is dissolved, and the strain relieved, when we give up the dream of a first philosophy firmer than science. If we are seeking only the causal mechanism of our knowledge of the external world, and not a justification of that knowledge in terms prior to science, we can settle after all for a theory of vision in Berkeley's style based on color patches in a two-dimensional visual field. The *Gestalt* psychologist may find that the threshold of awareness hovers somewhere in a misty mid-region of structured wholes; that remains an interesting point in its way, but we need not be put off by it. We can look upon man as a black box in the physical world, exposed to externally determinable stimulatory forces as input and spouting externally determinable testimony about the external world as output. Just which of the inner workings of the black box may be tinged with awareness is as may be.

Once we recognize the datum thus single-mindedly as what is closest to the physical stimulation, we find a strangely faithful realization of sensory atomism in the discreteness of the sensory nerve endings. Fire one afferent nerve and chalk up one sensory atom, and awareness be hanged. Ironically, though, it is just here that we do best at last to drop the talk of sense data and talk of nerve endings instead. Irony number four.

The threshold of awareness retains its importance too, but the conflict is gone; there are simply two levels to distinguish. The nerve endings, on the one hand, are the place of input of unprocessed information about the world. The stage where this information has become processed to the point of awareness, on the other hand, is the basic level for conceptualization and vocabulary. This is where observation flourishes—socially communicable and corroborable observation. It is the level that matters when in adjudicating a scientific theory we push the evidence back to observation. At the one level we do well, I suggested, to speak not of sense data but of nerve endings. At this other level we do well to speak not of sense data but of observation sentences.

Observation sentences at their strictest are sentences that we learned to use, or could have learned to use, by direct conditioning to socially shared concurrent stimulation. Typically they are sentences about external things, not sense data. What makes them so decisive in adjudicating scientific theories is that all speakers of the language who are present and attentive when an observation sentence is affirmed are apt to agree in assenting to the sentence or to agree in dissenting from it. They are sentences that anyone, nearly enough, who understands the language can verify or falsify by observation on the spot.

Why there are such sentences is no mystery. Any mystification about absolute certainty and incorrigibility, or about absolute immediacy of experience, can at this point be dismissed along with the dream of a first philosophy. To appreciate the

nature and origin of observation sentences we have only to reflect upon the ostensive process by which we learn many terms,
or one-word sentences. We learn them by hearing them used in
the presence of appropriate stimulations publicly shared, and
we are confirmed in our use of them by public approval in
the presence of similar stimulations. A term or sentence that
all speakers of the language, nearly enough, have learned in
this way, will qualify as an observation sentence. They are
sentences that members of the community are not apt to be
led to disagree over by differences in their previous experiences
or in their theoretical speculations.

Observation sentences can also run longer than a word, which,
anyway, is an ill-defined unit. Furthermore, an observation sentence may have been learned in the ostensive way only by some
speakers and in other ways by others. What distinguishes it is
just that the general usage of it conforms to concurrent observation in about the way that it would if everyone had learned it
ostensively. This conformity is what qualifies the observation
sentence for its crucial role in conveying evidence.

Observation sentences are crucial in two enterprises: in the
conveying of evidence and in the learning of a language. Such
sentences are necessarily our entering wedge into our first language; for clearly we can begin only by connecting heard utterances with concurrent stimulation, and by being confirmed in our
utterances by speakers who share the concurrent stimulation.

Unlike the earlier notion of datum, the notion of an observation sentence is rather clear and clean-cut. I already stated the
behavioral criterion that qualifies a sentence as an observation
sentence. It is just that all speakers of the language who are
present and attentive when such a sentence is affirmed are apt
to agree in assenting to the sentence or to agree in dissenting
from it. Someone may want to qualify the definition so as to
exclude sentences that everyone would assent to, or everyone
would dissent from, independently of concurrent stimulation;
but this is an easy emendation.

Ironically enough—and here is my fifth irony—some iconoclastic philosophers of science have taken to questioning the notion of observation only now that it ceases to present a problem. Theirs is, I think, a delayed reaction against the dubiety of the old notion of datum. Now that we have thrown off the old dream of a first philosophy, let us exult rather in our new access to unproblematical concepts. Neural input is one, and observation sentence as just now defined is another.

The criticism leveled against the notion of observation is that observation varies with the observer's interest and training. But I suggest that this variation is arrested when we define observation sentence by reference to the linguistic community as we have. We need only take a wide enough community and think of the sentence as tried on the community for assent and dissent in enough situations. The scientist will in practice apply the word 'observation' to conclusions involving tacit inference, but these shortcuts present no problem. Observations in this looser sense can be pushed back to observations in a more pedantic sense by continued challenge.

The quality of being an observation sentence does, strictly speaking, admit of degrees. Thus we may allow for one speaker's failure to agree with other speakers in assenting to an observation sentence on some occasion; we may simply take the degree of rarity of such exceptions into consideration in assessing how observational the sentence is. In further refinement of the notion, we may allow a speaker to revoke his assent to an observation sentence, or to revoke his dissent, after additional stimulation. Thus someone might assent to the one-word observation sentence 'Water' on the strength of an ocular stimulation, but change his verdict after detecting the odor of alcohol or gasoline. The degree of observationality of a sentence might then be measured inversely by the average dose of stimulation needed to induce a stable verdict.

All of us learn the use of many observation sentences ostensively, and any observation sentence could be learned ostensively. Or, allowing for degrees of observationality, we may put the point thus: the more observational a sentence is, the more nearly its use can be mastered ostensively. I mean 'ostensively' broadly here; it need not involve actual pointing. It is just that we learn under what total stimulatory situations to assent to the sentence, if asked, and under what stimulatory situations to dissent from it. This pair of classes of stimulatory situations—the class of favorable situations and the class of unfavorable ones—is the *stimulus meaning* of the observation sentence in question. The one class is the affirmative stimulus meaning, and the other the negative.

Rather than risk prejudicing matters by tendentious selections, I like to think of each of the stimulatory situations as total; the whole scene, in the visual case. The scenes in the affirmative stimulus meaning of the observation sentence 'Water' will all show water or a reasonable facsimile; and they will all show it conspicuously near the center of the visual field, sometimes pointed at and sometimes not.

We all have a sympathetic way of putting ourselves in the other fellow's place and sensing how the world would look from where he sits. This faculty is important in the dissemination of language. We see what way he is looking when he says 'Water' or assents to it. We emulate him when we find ourselves similarly oriented. He then checks the accuracy of our usage by noting our orientation. Such, with or without pointing, is the ostensive learning of an observation sentence.

This learning process depends, like any, on a prior sense of similarity, a sense of subjectively natural kinds. We volunteer or assent to the observation sentence 'Water,' in some stimulatory situation, and expect the other fellow's approval of our progress in the language, only because this stimulatory situation seems *like* the one that he was enjoying when he said 'Water' or assented to it. This scene, like the one he was enjoying, was all wet in the middle, and this wetness seemed much of a sameness from one scene to the other. You cannot learn, ostensively, a term or observation sentence with just any stimulus meaning. The term to be taught must have a stimulus meaning that hangs together according to the learner's subjective standards of similarity. You could not even learn a proper name like 'the Washington Monument' or 'the Taj Mahal' by ostension, if your subjective standard of similarity did not link earlier glimpses of the monument in question with later ones.

This learning process is a process of induction. The other fellow has affirmed or assented to the observation term or sentence in question, or has approved our assent to it, amid various scenes that were somewhat similar to one another; and we predict that he will do likewise in similar scenes hereafter. The similarity is similarity by our lights. Our learning of language thus depends heavily on the happy circumstance that similarity by our lights and similarity by the other fellow's lights go pretty much hand in hand.

The generality reached by our induction is rather a habit than a law, since we do not have words to state it with; we are only then engaged in learning to put a word to the generality in question. What we learn by the induction is the full range of scenes, or stimulatory situations, to which the word is appropriate—in short, its stimulus meaning.

I have been speaking of the observation sentence half the time as a word or term. In the case of 'Water' all three epithets are appropriate. The term 'water,' characteristically, is a mass term. In the full sophistication of our knowledge of the external world we may think of this term as designating that single spatiotemporally discontinuous but concrete object which consists of all the water ever. No matter that the stimulus meaning of the term consists rather of full scenes, or stimulus situations, and not just their aqueous portions. For it is quite right that the meaning of a term should differ from its designation. It is enough that the one determine the other, and indeed it does. Because the full scenes in the stimulus meaning of 'Water' ring all possible changes in their nonaqueous portions, they determine the aqueous designation unequivocally.

In treating a mass term thus as naming a scattered concrete object, I assimilate it to the singular term or proper name. 'Water' and 'sugar' join up with 'the Taj Mahal' and 'the Washington

Monument.' Actually these terms are much alike from the point of view of stimulus meaning. The scenes that feature the Washington Monument are scattered discontinuously along our stimulatory history, as are the scenes that feature water; and we assemble them under a single term by the same sort of similarity considerations.

I have been speaking of these observation terms as at once terms and sentences. Rendered as a full grammatical sentence, 'Water' amounts to 'This is water,' 'There is water here.' Conversely, the observation sentence 'It is raining' could be equated to the mass term 'rain'; and this term could be taken as naming the whole spatiotemporally discontinuous portion of the atmosphere that is occupied by rainfall. The full assimilation of observation sentences to singular terms can indeed prove artificial at points, and there is no purpose in pressing it except to suggest that a distinction between observation sentences and observation terms is inconsequential.

It remains inconsequential, however, only so long as we keep to singular terms, including mass terms. 'Rabbit,' or 'That is a rabbit,' is a good observation term or sentence, but as an observation term it should be taken only as a mass term, applying collectively to so much of the world as is made up of rabbit. It is only thus that the stimulus meaning suffices to fix the designatum. The stimulus meaning of 'Rabbit' consists, in its affirmative and visual part, of just those scenes that give noticeable evidence of rabbit presence. There is nothing in the stimulus meaning to fix 'Rabbit' as an individuative term, a term of divided reference; nothing to say how much to count as one rabbit and how much as two. Rabbits come discontinuously, yes, but so does water. Individuation is a big step, carrying us to another grade of theoreticity. Let us rest yet a while where we are, amid the mass terms and other singular terms of observational kind. I want to consider how much scientific theory one could aspire to at this primitive level.

Consider first the derivation of concepts, or, as I prefer to say, the compounding of terms. The terms 'red' and 'wine' would be at hand as observation terms. In our ontological sophistication, which of course might not be shared at the primitive conceptual level which we are imagining, the mass terms 'red' and 'wine' can be viewed as names each of an appropriate spatiotemporally scattered portion of the world. The compound term 'red wine,' then, called an *attributive compound,* designates that portion of the world which is the common part of the two. It again is an observation term, or observation sentence, and could be learned as a whole in the regular ostensive way, after the manner of 'red' and 'wine' themselves.

A man would not have to go through the ostensive learning of many such triads of observation terms—a term '*A*,' a term '*B*,' and an attributive compound '*AB*' for the common part of *A* and *B*—before he would catch on to the trick, and proceed to form all further attributive compounds on his own. Here, then, is a primitive bit of grammar at the level of observation terms.

Since the designatum of the term 'red wine' is the common part of the designata of 'red' and 'wine,' one might guess that the affirmative stimulus meaning of 'red wine' is likewise the common part of the affirmative stimulus meanings of 'red' and 'wine.' However, this is wrong. A stimulatory situation featuring white wine and a red apple belongs jointly to the affirmative stimulus meanings of 'red' and 'wine' but yet not to that of 'red wine.' Thus by taking the common part of these two stimulus meanings we get a stimulus meaning for some new compound of 'red' and 'wine,' not to be confused with the attributive compound 'red wine.' This new compound is best formulated in sentential form: 'Red here and wine here.'

This sentence, by the way, is not one that can usefully double as a mass term. There is a good sense in which 'red and wine' can be taken as a mass term, but it does not correspond to 'Red here and wine here.' The mass term 'red and wine' designates just so much of the world as is red or wine or both; what Goodman calls the fusion of red and wine. But its affirmative stimulus meaning is not the common part of those of 'red' and 'wine'; it is rather the union of those of 'red' and 'wine.' 'Red and wine,' in this sense, may properly be assented to whenever the scene features wine or anything red; 'Red here and wine here' may properly be assented to only when the scene features both wine and something red; and 'Red wine' may properly be assented to only when some of the wine is itself red.

We just saw that taking the common part of the designata is different from taking the common part of the affirmative stimulus meanings. A similar point can be made about complementation. The term 'unred' designates, we may say, the whole of the unred world. Its affirmative stimulus meaning will still include a scene that features something red, so long as it features something else too. The affirmative stimulus meaning complementary to that of 'red,' on the other hand, is the negative stimulus meaning of 'red'; its scenes feature nothing red. This meaning, again, is best expressed in sentential form: 'Red not here.'

We have noted two truth functions of observation sentences: the conjunction 'Red here and wine here' and the negation 'Red not here.' We have contrasted these with the two analogous mereological functions: the common part, red wine, and the complement, unred. The truth functions trade upon common parts and complements of stimulus meanings, and this, we saw, is not like taking common parts and complements of designata. When we move to alternation, however, we suddenly get a different story: the analogues converge. The mass term 'red and wine,' which we lately viewed as designating the fusion of red and wine, has as its positive stimulus meaning precisely the union of those of 'red' and 'wine.' Pooling designata *is* like pooling stimulus meanings; the mass term 'red and wine' and the alternation 'Red here or wine here' do come to the same thing.

Does it seem odd, in view of DeMorgan's law, that the analogues should thus converge in the case of alternation and yet diverge in the case of conjunction? Odd but not absurd; for there is the divergence also in the case of negation.

It should not be supposed that the modes of composition of terms or sentences that I have just now been canvassing are the only ones in this observation language. Such terms as 'cat on

mat' and a host of others are eligible. Some of these might con-
veniently be treated, despite appearances, as single and unanalyz-
able words learned ostensively as wholes. Others might invite
analysis, and this would mean recognizing and examining certain
additional modes of composition, though of course not yet going
so far as to recognize individuative terms as such. My reason
for singling out attributive composition, complementation, and
the truth functions for special treatment was just that these
modes of composition are of peculiarly logical and philosophical
concern.

The attributive compound 'red wine,' we noted, could have
been learned ostensively as a single word. If the same could be
said of all attributive compounds, and of the further kinds of
compounds that we have been considering, then these modes
of composition would conduce only to speed and not enrich-
ment. I feel confident, however, that this is not true. The question hinges on that subjective quality of similarity upon which
the ostensive learning of an observation term depends. Are all
unred stimulations felt to be sufficiently akin so that one could
learn the use of 'unred' outright as a simple word, independently of 'red,' by generalizing from a lot of ostensions? And
how about 'red and wine' in the alternational sense in which it
applies to all that is red or wine? The question is, in Goodman's
terminology, whether the terms 'unred' and 'red and wine' are
projectible. One inclines more strongly to a negative answer in
the case of such compounds than in the case of the attributive
compounds.

Hence I see these modes of composition of observation terms
as representing already a step upward in the theoreticity scale,
but a short one. In the case of the truth functions we can picture
how we might learn the step from our elders. We would notice
little by little that our elders were prepared to assent to the
negation of a sentence on just the occasions on which they
were prepared to dissent from the sentence, and vice versa. We
would notice further that they were prepared to assent to a conjunction on just the occasions on which they were prepared to

assent to each component; and that they were prepared to dissent from an alternation on just the occasions on which they were prepared to dissent from each component.

We have been considering the derivation of concepts at or near the observational level. What now of the discovery of laws of nature at that level? Simple induction is at our disposal. It has already been hard at work, however inarticulately, in our ostensive learning of observation terms. But what now of an induction at this level that uses terms 'A' and 'B' already learned, rather than just contributing to the learning of them? The result of the induction might be that the designatum of the mass term 'A,' in short the mass A, is part of B. Carmine is, in this sense, part of red. Both words have been learned by ostension, and the inclusion is reached inductively. Now this example would of course be regarded as part still of the ostensive learning of the term 'A' or 'carmine,' and not as a subsequent induction involving terms previously learned.

I think moreover that the induction would be similarly viewed even if, instead of A's being part of B, it were a matter merely of A's being always compresent with B. The affirmative stimulus meaning of the term 'A,' that is, is a subclass of the affirmative stimulus meaning of 'B,' and it is this inclusion that transpires inductively. I think still that we would regard this induction as part of the ostensive learning of the term 'A,' rather than as a subsequent induction. The presence of the mass or quality B would simply be felt as one of the various criteria by which we have learned, ostensively, to assent to 'A.'

For an induction that would naturally be regarded as truly subsequent to the learning of its terms, perhaps we must move to such a generalization as that wax melts in fire. The affirmative stimulus meaning of the observation term 'wax in fire' is, according to this generalization, a subclass of the affirmative stimulus meaning of the observation term 'wax melting'; insofar, the relation is like that of 'A' to 'B' in the preceding examples. But what saves this example is that 'wax in fire' is a compound, we may suppose, of prior observation terms 'wax' and 'fire,' rather than a simple term that was learned ostensively as a whole. Composition has intervened. I have an idea that the only difference between term-learning inductions and subsequent inductions, here at the level of observational discourse, is this intervention of one or more steps of composition of some sort. This makes the difference depend on how a given term was learned—whether ostensively as a whole or by composition of prior terms. That, however, is quite in order, since induction is in any event a way of learning.

I have said nothing about the vocabulary in which to state the results of inductions, here at the level of observational discourse. It would have to be added, acquired somehow, perhaps in less evident ways than we noted in the case of the truth functions. But inductions can be made, and can persist in the form of dispositions to action, even when not articulated. As remarked earlier, in fact, the ostensive learning of an observation term is itself just such an unarticulated induction.

The full apparatus for expressing generalities is quantification, or the equivalent. This goes far beyond what would be needed for expressing any generalities reached by induction from observation sentences. It marks a substantially higher grade of theoreticity. But there is also an intermediate grade to pause over, which is marked by Ruth Marcus' *substitutional* variant of quantification.

Construed in the substitutional way, a universal quantification '$(x)Fx$' is true just in case all sentences are true that can be got from 'Fx' by substituting for 'x,' and an existential quantification $(\exists x)Fx$' is true just in case some sentence thus obtainable is true. Substitutional quantification differs from regular quantification, what I call objectual quantification, in that '$(x)Fx$' in the substitutional sense does not say that *everything* x fulfills 'Fx,' but only everything for which a name is available. Correspondingly for the existential. Moreover, substitutional quantification makes sense also when the quantified position 'x' is not a position for names of anything; it makes sense when the expressions to be substituted for 'x' are expressions of any chosen grammatical category. Thus there is no special connection between substitutional quantification and objective reference to values of variables. Still, substitutional quantification resembles objectual quantification strongly enough to mark an instructive intermediate grade of theoreticity.

It would not be easy, in observing a people who spoke in quantifiers, to tell whether their quantification was substitutional or objectual. We would find, by observing their utterances and by putting various sentences to them for assent or dissent, that in general they were disposed to assent to an existential quantification in any circumstances in which they were prepared to assent to an instance of the quantification. We would find also that they were prepared to dissent from a universal quantification whenever prepared to dissent from an instance. This much is compatible with both the substitutional and the objectual interpretation of the quantifiers.

We cannot decide between these interpretations by considering whether the people are disposed to assent to an existential quantification *only* when prepared to assent to an instance. We would find they are not; we would find that they sometimes will assent to an existential quantification but to none of its instances. We would find this even if their quantification is substitutional. We would find them assenting to the quantification 'someone is in the next room' but unprepared to assent to any instance of the form 'x is in the next room,' and the reason is not that their quantification is objectual, but only that without looking in the next room they do not know what name to substitute. Similar remarks apply on the universal side; the people would be disposed sometimes to dissent from a universal quantification and yet to dissent from no one of its instances, but this again does not show their quantification to be objectual.

When we find them quantifying over individually nameless things such as electrons or grains of sand, we can in good conscience take their quantification as objectual rather than substitutional. It would be farfetched at this point to defend the substitutional interpretation on the ground that each grain of sand is in principle specifiable by its positional co-ordinates. In the case of electrons such a suggestion is even dubious in theory. If finally we find the people quantifying even over irrational numbers, and accepting Cantor's proof that some irrational numbers are individually unspecifiable, then the case for the objectual interpretation is as emphatic as it can be.

Objectual quantification and individuative terms go hand in hand. These terms are also called predicates, general terms, terms of divided reference. They play the role of the 'F' in the schema 'Fx.' Quantification is what gives significance to the schema 'Fx,' by distinguishing between the roles of the 'F' and the 'x.' The distinctive thing about the 'x' position is that it takes a variable of quantification; and the distinctive thing about an individuative term or predicate, then, is that it builds the 'x' out to a sentence 'Fx,' which can receive a quantifier.

The 'x' position in 'Fx' admits both variables and names; thus we may have 'Fa,' schematizing the contrast between general term and singular term, or predicate and subject. But this contrast exists only by virtue of variables and their quantifiers. What distinguishes the singular term from the general term is precisely that it belongs in the position of a variable of objectual quantification.

Might we not say also that the name is distinguished by its reference, by its designating something? But this raises the question what expressions to regard as designating things, and why; whether to regard general terms in turn as designating classes, for instance, or perhaps attributes. It is only the advent of the objectual quantifier and its variable, or the advent anyway of idioms to the same effect, that lends substance to the distinction between regarding an expression as a name and not so regarding it. The quantifier quantifies over the denizens of the chosen universe, and its variable takes those denizens as its values. A constant term is a name of one of those denizens if, whenever we put a variable 'x' for that term in any true sentence, the resulting open sentence is true of that denizen as value of 'x.'

If a language has only substitutional quantification or none, if we have no objectual quantification and no plan for defining it, then there is nothing recognizable as talk of objects; the question what there is does not arise. This is true in particular of the sort of observation language that we considered earlier. In that connection I talked of mass terms as naming portions of the world; however, that sort of talk made sense to us only because of our own more theoretical language with its quantifiers or equivalent devices. It was an interpretation of an anontological language in an ontological language.

The grade of theoreticity marked by objectual quantification is thus a notable grade indeed. It is where talk of things sets in; things, objects, entities. It is the grade of theoreticity that brings variables, and the values of the variables are what there are said to be. Even if we practice restraint on this score, accepting as values of the variables only physical objects of sensible magnitude, still we are operating at a theoretical level that is pretty high off the ground of observation. It is a grade of theoreticity adequate to common sense and historiography and natural history. It recognizes no numbers or sets or other abstract objects. Still, at this level you can simulate about enough elementary set theory to cover what is useful in the common man's references to classes. You can do this by what I call the virtual theory of classes; seeming references to classes are explained away by contextual definition. Moreover, while not recognizing numbers as objects you can still make sense of practical arithmetic at the elementary level, again exploiting tricks of contextual definition. The mathematical equipment thus available is very meager, but the mathematical requirements of historiography and natural history are modest.

Most of us would be greatly relieved, I think, if we could see our way to a systematic account of the world at this level. It is the quest of system and simplicity that has kept driving the scientist to posit further entities as values of his variables. The classical example is the kinetic theory of gases. Viewed in terms of gross bodies, Boyle's law of gases was a quantitative description of the behavior of pressurized chambers. By positing molecules, the law could be assimilated into a general theory of bodies in motion. Subsequent advances in physics have kept prompting the positing of further and further, smaller and smaller particles—sometimes as a means of actually simplifying previous theory, as in the kinetic theory of gases, and sometimes only as a means of accommodating new observations without too much loss of simplicity. Increasingly serious use of mathematics has been called for by these developments, and meanwhile the mathematicians have also been doing, on their own, the same trick as the physicists: multiplying entities, positing ever weirder species in order to simplify theory. Classical examples were the positing of ratios to make division generally applicable, the positing of negative numbers to make subtraction generally applicable, and the positing of irrationals and finally imaginaries to make exponentiation generally applicable. Less classical examples are burgeoning in the theory of infinite sets. Man's drive for system and simplicity leads, it seems, to ever new complexities. This is irony number six, and the greatest of them all.

Nelson Goodman
Seven Strictures on Similarity

SIMILARITY, I submit, is insidious. And if the association here with invidious comparison is itself invidious, so much the better. Similarity, ever ready to solve philosophical problems and overcome obstacles, is a pretender, an impostor, a quack. It has, indeed, its place and its uses, but is more often found where it does not belong, professing powers it does not possess.

The strictures I shall lay against similarity are none of them new, but only recently have I come to realize how often I have encountered this false friend and had to undo his work.

First Stricture: Similarity does not make the difference between representations and descriptions, distinguish any symbols as peculiarly 'iconic', or account for the grading of pictures as more or less realistic or naturalistic.[1]

The conviction that resemblance is the necessary and sufficient condition for representation is so deeply ingrained that the evident and conclusive arguments to the contrary are seldom considered. Yet obviously one dime is not a picture of another, a girl is not a representation of her twin sister, one printing of a word is not a picture of another printing of it from the same type, and two photographs of the same scene, even from the same negative, are not pictures of each other.

All that this proves, of course, is that resemblance alone is not enough for representation. But where reference has been established—where a symbol does refer to some object—is not similarity then a sufficient condition for the symbol's being a representation? Plainly *no.* Consider a page of print that begins with "the final seven words on this page" and ends with the same seven words repeated. The first of these seven-word inscriptions surely refers to the second, and is as much like it as can be, yet is no more a picture of it than is any printing of a word a picture of another printing.

1. See further *Languages of Art* (hereinafter *LA*) (Indianapolis and New York, 1968), chap. i.

Still, once pictures are somehow distinguished from other denotative symbols—and this must be by some other means than similarity—does not comparative naturalism or realism among pictures depend upon their degree of resemblance to what they represent? Not even this can be maintained. For pictures of goblins and unicorns are quite easily graded as more or less realistic or naturalistic or fantastic, though this cannot depend upon degree of resemblance to goblins and unicorns.

The most we can say is that among pictures that represent actual objects, degree of realism correlates to some extent with degree of similarity of picture to object. But we must beware of supposing that similarity constitutes any firm, invariant criterion of realism; for similarity is relative, variable, culture-dependent. And even where, within a single culture, judgments of realism and of resemblance tend to coincide, we cannot safely conclude that the judgments of realism follow upon the judgments of resemblance. Just the reverse may be at least equally true: that we judge the resemblance greater where, as a result of our familiarity with the manner of representation, we judge the realism greater.

Second Stricture: Similarity does not pick out inscriptions that are 'tokens of a common type', or replicas of each other.[2]

Only our addiction to similarity deludes us into accepting similarity as the basis for grouping inscriptions into the several letters, words, and so forth. The idea that inscriptions of the same letter are more alike than inscriptions of different letters evaporates in the glare of such counterexamples as those in Figure 1. One might argue that what counts is not degree of similarity

Figure 1

a	*d*	A
m	*w*	M

2. See further *The Structure of Appearance* (hereinafter *SA*), 2nd edition (Indianapolis and New York, 1966), pp. 360–364, and *LA*, pp. 131–141.

but rather similarity in a certain respect. In what respect, then, must inscriptions be alike to be replicas of one another? Some who should know better have supposed that the several inscriptions of the same letter are topologically equivalent, but to show how wrong this is we need only note that the first inscription in Figure 2 is not topologically equivalent to the second, and that the second mark in Figure 3 is topologically equivalent not to the first but to the third.

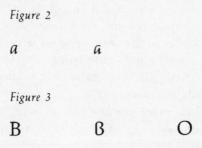

Figure 2

a   *ɑ*

Figure 3

B   ß   O

We have terrible trouble trying to say how two inscriptions must be alike to be replicas of one another—how an inscription must resemble other inscriptions of the letter *a* to be itself an *a*. I suspect that the best we can do is to say that all inscriptions that are *a*'s must be alike in being *a*'s. That has the solid ring of assured truth, but is hardly electrifying. Moreover, notice that to say that all *a*'s are alike in being *a*'s amounts simply to saying that all *a*'s are *a*'s. The words "alike in being" add nothing; similarity becomes entirely superfluous.

Third Stricture: Similarity does not provide the grounds for accounting two occurrences performances of the same work, or repetitions of the same behavior or experiment.[3]

In other words, what I have said about replicas of inscriptions applies also to events. Two performances of the same work may

3. See further *LA*, chap. IV.

be very different. Repetitions of the same behavior, such as hitting a tennis ball against a barn door, may invoke widely varying sequences of motions. And if we experiment twice, do the differences between the two occasions make them different experiments or only different instances of the same experiment? The answer, as Sir James Thomson stresses, is always relative to a theory[4]—we cannot repeat an experiment and look for a covering theory; we must have at least a partial theory before we know whether we have a repetition of the experiment. Two performances are of the same symphony if and only if, however unlike they may be, they comply with the same score. And whether two actions are instances of the same behavior depends upon how we take them; response to the command, "Do that again," may well be the question: "Do what again? Swat another fly or move choreographically the same way?"

In each of these cases, the grouping of occurrences under a work or an experiment or an activity depends not upon a high degree of similarity but upon the possession of certain characteristics. In the case of performances of a Beethoven symphony, the score determines what those requisite characteristics are; in the case of repetitions of an experiment, the constitutive characteristics must be sought in the theory or hypothesis being tested; in the case of ordinary actions, the principle of classification varies with our purposes and interests.

Fourth Stricture: Similarity does not explain metaphor or metaphorical truth.[5]

Saying that certain sounds are soft is sometimes interpreted as saying in effect that these sounds are like soft materials. Metaphor is thus construed as elliptical simile, and metaphorical truths as elliptical literal truths. But to proclaim that certain tones are soft because they are like soft materials, or blue because they are like blue colors, explains nothing. Anything is in some way

4. See "Some Thoughts on Scientific Method" in *Boston Studies in the Philosophy of Science,* vol. ii, ed. R. S. Cohen and Marx W. Wartofsky (New York, 1965), p. 85.

5. See further *LA,* pp. 68–80.

like anything else; any sounds whatever are like soft materials or blue colors in one way or another. What particular similarity does our metaphor affirm? More generally, what resemblance must the objects a term metaphorically applies to bear to the objects it literally applies to?

I do not think we can answer this question much better than we can answer the question what resemblance the objects a term literally applies to must bear to each other. In both cases, a reversal in order of explanation might be appropriate: the fact that a term applies, literally or metaphorically, to certain objects may itself constitute rather than arise from a particular similarity among those objects. Metaphorical use may serve to explain the similarity better than—or at least as well as—the similarity explains the metaphor.

Fifth Stricture: Similarity does not account for our predictive, or more generally, our inductive practice.[6]

That the future will be like the past is often regarded as highly dubious—an assumption necessary for science and for life but probably false, and capable of justification only with the greatest difficulty if at all. I am glad to be able to offer you something positive here. All these doubts and worries are needless. I can assure you confidently that the future will be like the past. I do not know whether you find this comforting or depressing. But before you decide on celebration or suicide, I must add that while I am sure the future will be like the past, I am not sure in just what way it will be like the past. No matter what happens, the future will be in some way like the past.

Let me illustrate. Suppose in investigating the relationship of two variables—say pressure and volume, or temperature and conductivity—for a given material, we obtain the data plotted as unlabelled dots in Figure 4. Where shall we expect the next point to be? Perhaps at a, since a is like all preceding points in falling on the same straight line. But b is like all earlier points in falling

---

6. See further *Fact, Fiction, and Forecast* (hereinafter *FFF*), 2nd edition (Indianapolis and New York, 1965), pp. 72–81, and *LA*, pp. 164–170.

Figure 4

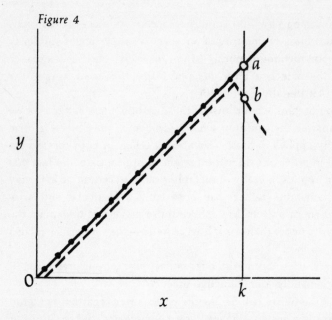

on the same curve (the broken line—and many others), and in fact *every* value of *y* where *x* = *k* will be like all earlier points in falling on some—and indeed many a—same curve.

Thus our predictions cannot be based upon the bald principle that the future will be like the past. The question is *how* what is predicted is like what has already been found. Along which among countless lines of similarity do our predictions run? I suspect that rather than similarity providing any guidelines for inductive practice, inductive practice may provide the basis for some canons of similarity.[7]

Sixth Stricture: Similarity between particulars does not suffice to define qualities.[8]

A good many good philosophers have supposed that, given particulars and a relation of likeness that obtains between two particulars if and only if they share at least one among certain

7. See FFF, pp. 121-122.

8. See further SA, pp. 145-149.

qualities, we can readily define such qualities and so avoid admitting them as additional undefined entities. If several particulars are all alike, the reasoning runs, they will all share some one quality or other; and qualities can thus be identified with the most comprehensive classes of particulars that are all alike.

The flaw here went unnoticed for a long time, simply for lack of logical scrutiny. Just how do we go from likeness between two particulars to likeness among several? Several particulars are all alike, we are tempted to say, if and only if each two of them are alike. But this will not work. Each two among three or more particulars may be alike (that is, have a quality in common) without all of them having any quality in common. Suppose, for example, we have three discs, the first one half red and half blue, the second one half blue and half yellow, and the third one half yellow and half red:

$$\begin{array}{ccc} rb & by & yr \\ 1 & 2 & 3 \end{array}$$

Each two of the three discs have a color in common, but there is no color common to all three. Dyadic likeness between particulars will not serve to define those classes of particulars that have a common quality throughout.

Seventh Stricture: Similarity cannot be equated with, or measured in terms of, possession of common characteristics.

This is a rather more general stricture, underlying some of the earlier ones.

When, in general, are two things similar? The first response is likely to be: "When they have at least one property in common." But since every two things have some property[9] in common, this will make similarity a universal and hence useless relation. That a given two things are similar will hardly be notable news if there are no two things that are not similar.

Are two things similar, then, only if they have all their prop-

9. Of course as a nominalist, I take all talk of properties as slang for more careful formulations in terms of predicates.

erties in common? This will not work either; for of course no two things have all their properties in common. Similarity so interpreted will be an empty and hence useless relation. That a given two things are similar in this sense would be notable news indeed, but false.

By now we may be ready to settle for a comparative rather than a categorical formula. Shall we say that two things a and b are more alike than two others c and d if a and b have more properties in common than do c and d? If that has a more scientific sound and seems safer, it is unfortunately no better; for any two things have exactly as many properties in common as any other two. If there are just three things in the universe, then any two of them belong together in exactly two classes and have exactly two properties in common: the property of belonging to the class consisting of the two things, and the property of belonging to the class consisting of all three things. If the universe is larger, the number of shared properties will be larger but will still be the same for every two elements. Where the number of things in the universe is n, each two things have in common exactly 2^{n-2} properties out of the total of $2^n - 1$ properties; each thing has 2^{n-2} properties that the other does not, and there are $2^{n-2}-1$ properties that neither has. If the universe is infinite, all these figures become infinite and equal.

I have, indeed, been counting only first-order extensional properties. Inclusion of higher-order properties will change the arithmetic but not the argument. The inevitable suggestion that we must consider intensional properties seems to me especially fruitless here, for identifying and distinguishing intensional properties is a notoriously slippery matter, and the idea of measuring similarity or anything else in terms of number of intensional properties need hardly be taken seriously.

More to the point would be counting not all shared properties but rather only *important* properties—or better, considering not the count but the overall importance of the shared properties. Then a and b are more alike than c and d if the cumulative importance of the properties shared by a and b is greater than that of the properties shared by c and d. But importance is a highly volatile matter, varying with every shift of context and interest, and quite incapable of supporting the fixed distinctions that philosophers so often seek to rest upon it.

Here, then, are seven counts in an indictment against similarity. What follows? First, we must recognize that similarity is relative and variable, as undependable as indispensable. Clear enough when closely confined by context and circumstance in ordinary discourse, it is hopelessly ambiguous when torn loose. In this, similarity is much like motion. Where a frame of reference is tacitly or explicitly established all is well; but apart from a frame of reference, to say that something moves is as incomplete as to say that something is to the left of. We have to say what a thing is to the left of, what it moves in relation to, and in what respects two things are similar.

Yet similarity, unlike motion, cannot be salvaged merely by recognizing its relativity. When to the statement that a thing moves we add a specification of the frame of reference, we remove an ambiguity and complete our initial statement. But when to the statement that two things are similar we add a specification of the property they have in common, we again remove an ambiguity; but rather than supplementing our initial statement, we render it superfluous. For, as we have already seen, to say that two things are similar in having a specified property in common is to say nothing more than that they have that property in common. Similarity is not definitionally eliminated here; we have neither a definiens serving as an appropriate replacement for every occurrence of "is similar to" nor a definitional schema that will provide an appropriate replacement for each occurrence. Rather we must search for the appropriate replacement in each case; and "is similar to" functions as little more than a blank to be filled.

Furthermore, comparative judgments of similarity often require not merely selection of relevant properties but a weighing of their relative importance, and variation in both relevance and importance can be rapid and enormous. Consider baggage at an airport check-in station. The spectator may notice shape, size, color, material, and even make of luggage; the pilot is more concerned with weight, and the passenger with destination and ownership. Which pieces of baggage are more alike than others depends not only upon what properties they share, but upon who makes the comparison, and when. Or suppose we have three glasses, the first two filled with colorless liquid, the third with a bright red liquid. I might be likely to say the first two are more like each other than either is like the third. But it happens that the first glass is filled with water and the third with water colored by a drop of vegetable dye, while the second is filled with hydrochloric acid—and I am thirsty. Circumstances alter similarities.

But have I overlooked the residual and most significant kind of similarity—similarity between qualities as measured by nearness of their positions in an ordering? We are no longer speaking of concrete things, with their countless properties, but of unidimensional qualities like hues or pitches. Is not such similarity free of variations resulting from different selections and weightings of relevant properties? Surely, pitches are the more alike as they differ by fewer vibrations per second. But are they? Or is middle C more like high C than like middle D? The question is argument enough. Similarity of so-called simple qualities can be measured by nearness of their positions in an ordering, but they may be ordered, with good reason, in many different ways.

What, then, shall we say of the orderings of sensory qualities as mapped by psychophysicists on the basis of paired comparisons, fractionations, matching, and so forth? If many such methods yield closely congruent maps, relative nearness of position on such a map amounts to similarity under the general conditions and in the general context of the laboratory experiments, and has good title to be taken as a standard measure of similarity among the qualities in question. But can we test the validity of the methods used by examining how well similarity so measured agrees with ordinary judgments of likeness? I think there is no satisfactory way of stabilizing ordinary, as against laboratory, conditions and context to obtain judgments of sensory similarity that are qualified to stand as criteria for appraising the laboratory results. The laboratory results create rather than reflect a measure of sensory similarity. Like most systems of measurement, they tend to govern ordinary judgments at least as much as to be governed by them. And we have seen that the relative weighting of the different qualities of objects is so variable that even reliable measures of similarity for qualities of each kind will give no constant measure of overall similarity for the objects themselves.

Relativity, even volatility, is not a fatal fault. Physics does not stop talking of motion merely because motion is not absolute. But similarity, as we have seen, is a much more slippery matter. As it occurs in philosophy, similarity tends under analysis either to vanish entirely or to require for its explanation just what it purports to explain.

You may feel deprived, depressed, or even angry at losing one more handy tool from the philosopher's dwindling kit. But the rejection of similarity is not, as in the case of classes, rejection of some logical hanky-panky on grounds of philosophical distaste, nor, as in the case of intensions, modalities, analyticity, and synonymy, the rejection of some philosophical tomfoolery on grounds of utter obscurity. If statements of similarity, like counterfactual conditionals and four-letter words, cannot be trusted in the philosopher's study, they are still serviceable in the streets.

P. F. Strawson
Imagination and Perception

*Psychologists have hitherto failed to realize that imagination is a necessary ingredient of perception itself.**

I

The uses, and applications, of the terms 'image,' 'imagine,' 'imagination,' 'imaginative,' and so forth make up a very diverse and scattered family. Even this image of a family seems too definite. It would be a matter of more than difficulty exactly to identify and list the family's members, let alone establish their relationships of parenthood and cousinhood. But we can at least point to different areas of association in each of which some members of this group of terms ordinarily find employment. Here are three such areas: (1) the area in which imagination is linked with *image* and image is understood as *mental image*—a picture in the mind's eye or (perhaps) a tune running through one's head; (2) the area in which imagination is associated with invention, and also (sometimes) with originality or insight or felicitous or revealing or striking departure from routine; (3) the area in which imagination is linked with false belief, delusion, mistaken memory, or misperception. My primary concern here is not with any of these three areas of association, though I shall refer to them all, and especially to the first. My primary topic is Kant's use of the term 'imagination,' in the *Critique of Pure Reason*, in connection with perceptual recognition—a use which may appear something of an outsider, but nevertheless has claims to affinity which are worth considering. I shall refer also to Hume and to Wittgenstein. My paper in general belongs to the species *loosely ruminative* and *comparative-historical* rather than to the species *strictly argumentative* or *systematic-analytical.*

* Immanuel Kant, *Critique of Pure Reason*, trans. Norman Kemp Smith (London, 1933), A120, fn.a.

II

Sometimes Kant used the term 'imagination' and its cognates in what is apparently a very ordinary and familiar way; as when, for example, he seems to contrast our imagining something with our having knowledge or experience of what is actually the case. Thus in a note in the "Refutation of Idealism" he writes: "It does not follow that every intuitive representation of outer things involves the existence of these things, for their representation can very well be the product *merely of the imagination* (as in dreams and delusions). . . . Whether this or that supposed experience be not *purely imaginary* must be ascertained from its special determinations, and through its congruence with the criteria of all real experience."[1] Sometimes, however, indeed more frequently, his use of the term seems to differ strikingly from any ordinary and familiar use of it, so that we are inclined to say he must be using it in a technical or specialized way of his own. Suppose, for example, that I notice a strange dog in the garden, and observe its movements for a while; and perhaps also notice, a few minutes later, that it is still there. We should not ordinarily say that this account of a small and uninteresting part of my history included the report of any exercise of the imagination on my part. Yet, in Kant's apparently technical use of the term, any adequate analysis of such a situation would accord a central role to imagination, or to some faculty entitled 'imagination.'

In both these respects there is a resemblance between Kant and Hume. That is to say, Hume, like Kant, sometimes makes an apparently ordinary use of the term (as when he is discussing the differences between imagination and memory) and sometimes makes an apparently technical use of it; and the latter use is such that he, too, like Kant, would say that imagination enters essentially into the analysis of the very ordinary situation I described a moment ago. It may be instructive to see how far this resemblance goes.

1. Kant, B278-9 (my italics).

Let us return to our simple situation. Both Hume and Kant would say (a) that my recognizing the strange dog I see as a dog at all owes something to the imagination; and (b) that my taking what I continuously, or interruptedly, observe to be the same object, the same dog, throughout, also owes something to the imagination. By both philosophers imagination is conceived as a connecting or uniting power which operates in two dimensions. In one dimension, (a), it connects perceptions of different objects of the same kind; in the other dimension, (b), it connects different perceptions of the same object of a given kind. It is the instrument of our perceptual appreciation both of kind-identity and of individual-identity, both of concept-identity and of object-identity. The two dimensions or varieties of connecting power are, doubtless, not independent of each other, but they can, to some extent, be handled separately. I begin by referring briefly to (a); then I treat more fully of (b); and then return in Section IV, below, to (a).

Kant's doctrine (or part of it) on (a) is sketched in the chapter on schematism, and Hume's in the chapter in the *Treatise* called "Of abstract ideas." Kant declares the schema to be a product of, and also a rule for, the imagination, in accordance with which, and by means of which alone, the imagination can connect the particular image or the particular object with the general concept under which it falls. Hume speaks, in his usual way, of the resemblance of particular ideas being the foundation of a customary association both among the resemblant particular ideas themselves and between them and the "annex'd" general term; so that the imagination is, or may be, ready with an appropriate response whenever it gets a cue, as it were, from anywhere in the associative network. How the mechanism is supposed exactly to work is not very clear either in the case of Hume or in that of Kant. But the obscurity of this very point is something which both authors emphasize themselves, in sentences which show a quite striking parallelism. Thus Kant says of schematism that it is "an art concealed in the depths of the human soul, whose real modes of activity nature is hardly likely ever to allow us to discover and have open to our gaze."[2] And Hume, speaking of the imagination's readiness with appropriate particular ideas, describes it as a "kind of magical faculty in the soul which, though it be always most perfect in the greatest geniuses, and is properly what we call a genius, is, however, inexplicable by the utmost efforts of human understanding."[3] Imagination, then, insofar as its operations are relevant to the application of the same general concept in a variety of different cases, is a concealed art of the soul, a magical faculty, something we shall never fully understand.

Let us turn now to (b), to the matter of different phases of experience being related to the same particular object of some general type. In both authors this question is absorbed into a larger one, though the larger question is somewhat differently conceived in each of them. The main relevant passages here are, in the *Critique,* the section on "Transcendental Deduction" and, in the *Treatise,* the chapter "Scepticism with Regard to the Senses." Let us begin with Hume.

Hume makes a threefold distinction between sense (or the senses), reason (or understanding), and imagination. His famous question about the causes which induce us to believe in the existence of body resolves itself into the question to which of these faculties, or to what combination of them, we should ascribe this belief, that is, the belief in the *continued* and *distinct* existence of bodies. Certainly, he says, not to the senses alone and unassisted. For "when the mind looks further than what immediately appears to it, its conclusions can never be put to the account of the senses";[4] and the mind certainly "looks further" than this, both in respect of the belief in the *continued* existence of objects when we are no longer, as we say, perceiv-

2. Kant, B180–1.

3. David Hume, *A Treatise of Human Nature,* ed. L. A. Selby-Bigge (Oxford, 1888), p. 24. Spelling and punctuation have been changed.

4. Hume, p. 189.

ing them and in respect of the obviously connected belief in the *distinctness* of their existence from that of our perceptions of them. Equally certainly, he says, we cannot attribute these beliefs to Reason, that is to reasoning based on perceptions. For the only kind of reasoning that can be in question here is reasoning based on experience of constant conjunction, or causal reasoning. But whether we conceive of objects as the same in kind as perceptions or as different in kind from perceptions, it remains true that "no beings are ever present to the mind but perceptions"[5] and all perceptions which are present to the mind are present to the mind;[6] hence it is equally certain that we can never observe a constant conjunction either between perceptions present to the mind and perceptions not present to the mind or between perceptions on the one hand and objects different in kind from perceptions on the other.

The belief in question, then, must be ascribed to the Imagination—or, more exactly, to the "concurrence" of some of the qualities of our impressions with some of the qualities of the imagination. And here Hume launches into that famous account of the operations of imagination which, on account of its perverse ingenuity, can scarcely fail to command admiration both in the original and the modern senses of the word. It runs roughly as follows: imagination engenders so strong a propensity to confound the similarity of temporally separated and hence nonidentical perceptions with strict identity through time that, in defiance of sense and reason combined, we feign, and believe in, a continued existence of perceptions where there is patently no such thing; and so strong is the hold of this belief that, when the discrepancy is pointed out, the imagination can still find an ally in certain philosophers who try, though vainly, to satisfy reason and imagination at the same time by conceiving of objects as different in kind from perceptions and ascribing continued

5. Hume, p. 212.

6. I modify at least the appearance of Hume's argument here. He seems to suppose that the required premise at this point has an *empirical* character.

existence to the former and interrupted existence only to the latter.

When we turn from Hume to Kant, it is probably the divergencies rather than the parallels which we find most striking in this case—at least at first. And perhaps we can come at these by considering a *simpliste* criticism of Hume. For Hume's account is full of holes. One of the most obvious relates to his bland assertion that the unreflective, as opposed to the philosophers, take the objects of perception to be of the same species as perceptions of those objects; so that the problem of accounting for the belief, in its *vulgar* form, in the continued existence of objects is the problem of accounting for a belief which reason shows to be ungrounded and ungroundable, namely a belief in the existence of perceptions which nobody has. Of course it is quite false that the vulgar make any such identification and hence quite false that they hold any such belief as Hume presumes to account for. The vulgar *distinguish,* naturally and unreflectively, between their seeings and hearings (perceivings) of objects and the objects they see and hear, and hence have no difficulty in reconciling the interruptedness of the former with the continuance of existence of the latter. Indeed these distinctions and beliefs are built into the very vocabulary of their perception-reports, into the concepts they employ, the meanings of the things they say, in giving (unsophisticated) accounts of their hearings and seeings of things. So Hume's problem does not really exist and his solution to it is otiose.

I think Kant would regard these criticisms as just, but would deny that there was therefore no problem at all for the philosopher. That is, he would agree that the problem was not, as Hume conceived it, that of accounting, on the basis of the character of our perceptual experience, for certain beliefs (beliefs in the continued and distinct existence of bodies). For he would agree that it would be impossible to give accurate, plain reports of our perceptual experience which did not already incorporate those beliefs. The beliefs form an essential part of the conceptual framework which has to be employed to give a candid and veridical description of our perceptual experience. But this does not mean that there is no question to be asked. Hume starts his investigation, as it were, too late; with perceptual experience already established in the character it has, he leaves himself no room for any such question as he wishes to ask. But we ought to ask, not how it can be that on the basis of perceptual experience as it is, we come to have the beliefs in question, but *how it is* that perceptual experience is already such as to embody the beliefs in question; or, perhaps better, *what* it is for perceptual experience to be such as to embody the beliefs in question.

I do not want to invoke more of the complex apparatus of the critical philosophy than is necessary to bring out the parallels with Hume that lie below or behind or beside the divergencies. We know that Kant thought that perceptual experience did not just *happen* to have the general character it has, but *had* to have at least something like this character, if experience (that is the temporally extended experience of a self-conscious being) was to be possible at all. Just now we are not so much concerned with the soundness of this view as with the question of what he thought was *involved* in perceptual experience having this character. One of the things he certainly thought was involved is this: "A combination of them [perceptions or representations], such as they cannot have in sense itself, is demanded."[7] And this "such as they cannot have in sense itself" arouses at least a faint echo of Hume's view that sense itself could never give rise to the *opinion* of the continued and distinct existence of body. The reason Hume gives for this view, it will be recalled, is that in embracing such an *opinion*, "the mind looks further than what immediately appears to it." Now could Kant have a *similar* reason for holding that, for the use of concepts of relatively permanent bodies (that is for perceptual experience to have the character it does have), a combination such as perceptions cannot have in sense itself is demanded?

I think he could have. For even when Hume is submitted to

7. Kant, A120.

the sort of correction I sketched above, there is *something* right about the phrase of his I have just quoted. When I naively report what I see at a moment (say, as a tree or a dog), my mind or my report certainly "looks further" than *something*—not, usually, than "what immediately appears to me" (tree or dog), but certainly further than the merely subjective side of the event of its immediately appearing to me. Of a fleeting perception, a subjective event, I give a description involving the mention of something not fleeting at all, but lasting, not a subjective event at all, but a distinct object. It is clear, contra Hume, not only that I *do* do this, but that I *must* do it in order to give a natural and unforced account of my perceptions. Still, there arises the question what is necessarily involved in this being the case. The uninformative beginnings of an answer consist in saying that one thing necessarily involved is our possession and application of concepts of a certain kind, namely concepts of distinct and enduring objects. But now, as both Kant and Hume emphasize, the whole course of our experience of the world consists of relatively transient and changing perceptions. (The changes, and hence the transience, may be due to changes in the scene or in our orientation, broadly understood, towards the scene.) It seems reasonable to suppose that there would be no question of applying concepts of the kind in question unless those concepts served in a certain way to *link* or *combine* different perceptions—unless, specifically, they could, and sometimes did, serve to link *different* perceptions as perceptions of the *same* object. Here, then, is one aspect of combination, as Kant uses the word, and just the aspect we are now concerned with. Combination, in this sense, is *demanded*. We could not count any transient perception as a perception of an enduring object of some kind unless we were prepared to count, and did count, some transient perceptions as, though different perceptions, perceptions of the same object of such a kind. The concepts in question could get no grip at all unless different perceptions were sometimes in this way combined by them. And when Kant says that this sort of combination of perceptions is such as they (the perceptions) cannot have in sense itself, we may perhaps take him to be making *at least* the two following unexceptionable, because tautological, points:

1) that this sort of combination is dependent on the possession and application of this sort of concept, that is, that if we did not *conceptualise* our sensory intake in this sort of way, then our sensory impressions would not be *combined* in this sort of way;

2) that distinguishable perceptions combined in this way, whether they are temporally continuous (as when we see an object move or change color) or temporally separated (as when we see an object again after an interval), really are distinguishable, that is different, perceptions.

Of course, in saying that we can find these two unexceptionable points in Kant's Hume-echoing dictum about combination, I am not for a moment suggesting that this account covers all that Kant means by combination; only that it may reasonably be taken to be included in what Kant means.

But now how does imagination come into the picture, that is into Kant's picture? Kant's problem, as we have seen, is not the same as Hume's; so he has no call to invoke imagination to do the job for which Hume invokes it, that is the job of supplementing actual perceptions with strictly imaginary perceptions which nobody has, which there is no reason to believe in the existence of and every reason not to believe in the existence of, but which we nevertheless *do* believe in the existence of as a condition of believing in the existence of body at all. This is not how imagination can come into Kant's picture. But certainly imagination *does* come into his picture; and the question is whether we can give any intelligible account of its place there. I think we can give some sort of account, though doubtless one that leaves out much that is mysterious in Kant and characteristic of him.

To do this we must strengthen our pressure at a point already touched on. We have seen that there would be no question of counting any transient perception as a perception of an enduring and distinct object unless we were prepared or ready to count some different perceptions as perceptions of one and the same enduring and distinct object. The thought of *other* actual or possible perceptions as related in this way to the *present* perception has thus a peculiarly intimate relation to our counting or taking—to our ability to count or take—this present perception as the perception of such an object. This is not of course to say that even when, for example, we perceive and recognize (re-identify as the object it is) a familiar particular object, there need occur anything which we would count as the experience of actually recalling any particular past perception of that object. (It is not in *this* way, either, that imagination comes into the picture.) Indeed the more familiar the object, the less likely any such experience is. Still, in a way, we can say in such a case that the past perceptions are *alive* in the present perception. For it would not be just the perception it is but for them. Nor is this just a matter of an external, causal relation. Compare seeing a face you *think* you know, but cannot associate with any previous encounter, with seeing a face you *know* you know and can very well so associate, even though there does not, as you see it, occur any particular *episode* of recalling any particular previous encounter. The comparison will show why I say that the past perceptions are, in the latter case, not merely causally operative, but alive in the present perception.

Of course when you first see a new, an unfamiliar thing of a familiar kind, there is no question of past perceptions of *that* thing being alive in the present perception. Still, one might say, to take it, to see it, as a thing of that kind is implicitly to have the thought of other possible perceptions related to your actual perception as perceptions of the same object. To see it as a dog, silent and stationary, is to see it as a possible mover and barker, even though you give yourself no actual images of it as moving and barking; though, again, you might do so if, say, you were particularly timid, if, as we say, your imagination was particularly active or particularly stimulated by the sight. Again, as you continue to observe it, it is not just a dog, with such and such characteristics, but *the* dog, the object of your recent observation, that you see, and see it as.

It seems, then, not too much to say that the actual occurrent perception of an enduring object as an object of a certain kind, or as a particular object of that kind, is, as it were, soaked with, or animated by, or infused with—the metaphors are *à choix*—the thought of other past or possible perceptions of the same object. Let us speak of past and merely possible perceptions alike as 'nonactual' perceptions. Now the imagination, in one of its aspects —the first I mentioned in this paper—is the image-producing faculty, the faculty, we may say, of producing actual representatives (in the shape of images) of nonactual perceptions. I have argued that an actual perception of the kind we are concerned with owes its character essentially to that internal link, of which we find it so difficult to give any but a metaphorical description, with other past or possible, but in any case nonactual, perceptions. Nonactual perceptions are in a sense represented in, alive in, the present perception; just as they are represented, by images, in the image-producing activity of the imagination. May we not, then, find a kinship between the capacity for this latter kind of exercise of the imagination and the capacity which is exercised in actual perception of the kind we are concerned with? Kant, at least, is prepared to register his sense of such a kinship by extending the title of 'imagination' to cover both capacities; by speaking of imagination as "a necessary ingredient of perception itself."

III

Suppose we so understand—or understand as including at least so much—the Kantian idea of the synthesis of imagination. The connection of the idea, so understood, with the application of concepts of objects is already clear. Can we also explain the introduction of the qualification 'transcendental'? If we bear in mind the opposition between 'transcendental' and 'empirical,' I think we can put two glosses on 'transcendental' here, both with a common root. First, then, we must remember the distinction between what Kant thought necessary to the possibility of any experience and what he thought merely contingently true of experience as we actually enjoy it. There is, in this sense, no necessity about our employment of the particular sets of empirical concepts we do employ, for example the concepts of elephant or ink bottle. All that is necessary is that we should employ some empirical concepts or other which exemplify, or give a footing to, those very abstractly conceived items, the categories, or concepts of an object in general. Synthesis, then, or the kind of exercise of the imagination (in Kant's extended sense) which is involved in perception of objects *as* objects, is empirical in one aspect and transcendental in another: it is empirical (that is nonnecessary) in so far as it happens to consist in the application of this or that particular empirical concept (elephant or ink bottle); transcendental (that is necessary) in so far as the application of such concepts represents, though in a form which is quite contingent, the utterly general requirements of a possible experience.

The second, connected, gloss we can put upon 'transcendental' can be brought out by comparison, once more, with Hume. Hume seems to think of the operations of imagination as something superadded to actual occurrent perceptions, the latter having a quite determinate character independent of and unaffected by the imagination's operations (though, of course, our *beliefs* are not unaffected by those operations). The Kantian synthesis, on the other hand, however conceived, is something necessarily involved in, a necessary condition of, actual occurrent reportable perceptions having the character they do have. So it may be called 'transcendental' in contrast with any process, for example any ordinary associative process, which presupposes a basis of actual, occurrent, reportable perceptions.

IV

Insofar as we have supplied anything like an explanation or justification of Kant's apparently technical use of 'imagination,' we have done so by suggesting that the recognition of an enduring object of a certain kind *as* an object of that kind, or as a certain particular object of that kind, involves a certain sort of connection with other nonactual perceptions. It involves other past (and hence nonactual) perceptions, or the thought of other possible (and hence nonactual) perceptions, of the *same* object being somehow alive in the present perception. The question arises whether we can stretch things a little further still to explain or justify the apparently technical use of 'imagination' in connection with our power to recognize *different* (and sometimes very different) particular objects as falling under the same general concept.

We can begin by making the platitudinous point that the possession of at least a fair measure of this ability, in the case, say, of the concept of a tree, is at least a test of our knowing what a tree is, of our possessing the concept of a tree. And we can progress from this to another point, both less platitudinous and more secure: namely, that it would be unintelligible to say of someone that whereas he could recognize *this* particular object as a tree, he could not recognize any other trees as trees.[8] So it would not make sense to say, in the case of a particular momentary perception, that he who had it recognized what he saw as a tree unless we were prepared also to ascribe to him the power of recognizing other things as well as trees. Now, how are we to regard this power or potentiality as related to his momentary perception? Is it just something external to it, or superadded to it, just an extra qualification he must possess, as it were, if his momentary perception is to count as a case of tree-recognition? This picture of the relation seems wrong. But if we say it *is* wrong,

8. Perhaps it is necessary to add that I do not mean that we could not conceive of any circumstances at all (for example, of mental disorder) in which this would be an apt thing to say.

if we say that the character of the momentary perception itself depends on the connection with this general power, then have we not in this case too the same sort of link between actual and nonactual perceptions (now of *other* things) as we had in the previously discussed case between actual and nonactual perceptions (then of the *same* thing)? But if so, then we have another reason, similar to the first reason though not the same as it, for saying that imagination, in an extended sense of the word, is involved in the recognition of such a thing as the sort of thing it is. Once more, this is not a matter of supposing that we give ourselves actual images, either of other trees perceived in the past or of wholly imaginary trees not perceived at all, whenever, in an actual momentary perception, we recognize something as a tree. It is not in this way, that is, by being represented by actual images, that nonactual (past or possible) perceptions enter into actual perception. They enter, rather, in that elusive way of which we have tried to give an account. But may we not here again, for this very reason, find a kinship between perceptual recognition (of an object as of a certain kind) and the more narrowly conceived exercise of the imagination—enough of a kinship, perhaps, to give some basis for Kant's extended use of the term 'imagination' in this connection too, and perhaps, this time, for Hume's as well?

V

It does not, of course, matter very much whether we come down in favor of, or against, this extended or technical application of the term 'imagination.' What matters is whether, in looking into possible reasons or justifications for it, we find that any light is shed on the notion of perceptual recognition. And here I want to summon a third witness. The third witness is Wittgenstein. I consider his evidence, first, in this section, without any reference to any explicit use, by him, of the term 'imagination'; then, in the next, I refer to some of his own uses of terms of this family.

On page 212 of the *Investigations* Wittgenstein says: "We find certain things about seeing puzzling because we do not find the whole business of seeing puzzling enough." This comes nearly at the end of those twenty pages or so which he devotes to the discussion of *seeing as*, of aspects and changes of aspect. Nearly all the examples he considers, as far as visual experience is concerned, are of pictures, diagrams, or signs, which can present different aspects, can be seen now as one thing, now as another. He is particularly impressed by the case where they undergo a change of aspects under one's very eyes, as it were, the case where one is suddenly struck by a new aspect. What, I think, he finds particularly impressive about this case is the very obviously *momentary* or *instantaneous* character of the being struck by the new aspect. Why does this impress him so much? Well, to see an aspect, in this sense, of a thing is, in part, to *think* of it in a certain way, to be disposed to *treat* it in a certain way, to give certain sorts of explanations or accounts of what you see, in general to *behave* in certain ways. But, then, how, he asks, in the case of seeing an aspect, is this thinking of the thing in a certain way related to the *instantaneous* experience? We could perhaps imagine someone able to *treat* a picture in a certain way, painstakingly to *interpret* it in that way, without *seeing* the relevant aspect, without seeing it *as* what he was treating it as, at all.[9] But this does not help us with the case of the instantaneous experience. It would be quite wrong to speak of this case as if there were merely an external relation, inductively established, between the thought, the interpretation, and the visual experience: to say, for example, that 'I see the x as a y' means 'I have a particular visual experience which I have found that I always have when I interpret the x as a y.'[10] So Wittgenstein casts around for ways of expressing himself which will hit off the relation. Thus we have: "The flashing of an aspect on us seems half visual experience, half

9. Ludwig Wittgenstein, *Philosophical Investigations*, trans. G. E. M. Anscombe (Oxford, 1953), pp. 204, 212, 213–214.

10. Wittgenstein, pp. 193–194.

thought";[11] or again, of a different case, "Is it a case of both seeing *and* thinking? or an amalgam of the two, as I should almost like to say?";[12] or again, of yet another, "It is almost as if 'seeing the sign in this context' [under this aspect] were an echo of a thought. 'The echo of a thought in sight'—one would like to say."[13]

Beside Wittgenstein's metaphor of "the echo of the thought in sight" we might put others: the visual experience is *irradiated* by, or *infused* with, the concept; or, it becomes *soaked* with the concept.

Wittgenstein talks mainly of pictures or diagrams. But we must all have had experiences like the following: I am looking towards a yellow flowering bush against a stone wall, but I see it as yellow chalk marks scrawled on the wall. Then the aspect changes and I see it normally, that is I see it as a yellow flowering bush against the wall. On the next day, however, I see it normally, that is I see it as a yellow flowering bush against the wall, all the time. Some persons, perhaps with better eyesight, might never have seen it as anything else, might always *see it as* this. No doubt it is only against the background of some such experience of change of aspects, or of the thought of its possibility, that it is quite natural and nonmisleading to speak, in connection with ordinary perception, of *seeing* objects *as* the objects they are. But this does not make it incorrect or false to do so generally.[14] Wittgenstein was perhaps *over*impressed by the cases where we are *suddenly* struck by something—be it a classical change of figure-aspects or the sudden recognition of a face or the sudden appearance of an object, as when an ordinary rabbit bursts into view in the landscape and captures our attention.[15]

11. Wittgenstein, p. 197.

12. Wittgenstein, p. 197.

13. Wittgenstein, p. 212.

14. Wittgenstein resists the generalization. See p. 197, " 'Seeing as' is not part of perception," and p. 195. But he also gives part of the reason for making it; see pp. 194–195.

15. Wittgenstein, p. 197.

Though there clearly are distinctions between cases, there are also continuities. There is no reason for making a sharp conceptual cleavage between the cases of a sudden irruption—whether of an aspect or an object—and others. We can allow that there are cases where visual experience is suddenly irradiated by a concept and cases where it is more or less steadily soaked with the concept. I quote once more: "We find certain things about seeing puzzling because we do not find the whole business of seeing puzzling enough." Perhaps we should fail less in this respect if we see that the striking case of the *change* of aspects merely dramatizes for us a feature (namely seeing as) which is present in perception in general.

Now how do we bring this to bear on Kant? Well, there is a point of analogy and a point of difference. The thought is echoed in the sight, the concept is alive in the perception. But when Wittgenstein speaks of *seeing as* as involving thinking-of-as, as involving the thought or the concept, he has in mind primarily a disposition to behave in certain ways, to treat or describe what you see in certain ways—such a disposition itself presupposing (in a favorite phrase) the mastery of a technique. This is the *criterion* of the visual experience, the means by which someone other than the subject of it must tell what it is. This, taking us on to familiar Wittgensteinian ground, gives us indeed a peculiarly intimate link between the momentary perception and something else; but the 'something else' is behavior, and so the upshot seems remote from the peculiarly intimate link we labored to establish in connection with Kant's use of the term 'imagination': the link between the actual present perception of the object and other past or possible perceptions of the same object or of other objects of the same kind. But is it really so remote? Wittgenstein's special preoccupations pull him to the behavioral side of things, to which Kant pays little or no attention. But we can no more think of the behavioral dispositions as merely externally related to *other* perceptions than we can think of them as merely externally related to the present perception. Thus the relevant behavior in reporting an aspect may be to point to *other* objects of *perception.*[16] Or in the case of seeing a real, as opposed to a picture-object, as a such-and-such, the behavioral disposition includes, or entails, a readiness for, or expectancy of, other perceptions, of a certain character, of the same object.

Sometimes this aspect of the matter—the internal link between the present and other past or possible perceptions—comes to the fore in Wittgenstein's own account. Thus, of the case of sudden recognition of a particular object, an old acquaintance, he writes: "I meet someone whom I have not seen for years; I see him clearly, but fail to know him. Suddenly I know him, *I see the old face in the altered one.*"[17] Again, he says of the dawning of an aspect: "What I perceive in the dawning of an aspect is . . . an internal relation between it [the object] and other objects."[18]

VI

I have mentioned the fact that there are points in these pages at which Wittgenstein himself invokes the notions of imagination and of an image. I shall discuss these points now. He first invokes these notions in connection with the drawing of a triangle, a right-angled triangle with the hypotenuse downmost and the right angle upmost. "This triangle," he says, "can be seen as a triangular hole, as a solid, as a geometrical drawing; as standing on its base, as hanging from its apex; as a mountain, as a wedge, as an arrow or pointer, as an overturned object which is meant to stand on the shorter side of the right angle, as a half-parallelogram and as various other things."[19] Later he reverts to this example and says: "The aspect of the triangle: it is as if an *image*

16. Cf. p. 194; and p. 207: "Those two aspects of the double cross might be reported simply by pointing alternately to an isolated white and an isolated black cross."

17. Wittgenstein, p. 197 (my italics).

18. Wittgenstein, p. 212.

19. Wittgenstein, p. 200.

came into contact, and for a time remained in contact, with the visual impression."[20] He contrasts some of the triangle-aspects in this respect with the aspects of some other of his examples; and a little later he says: "It is possible to take the duck-rabbit simply for the picture of a rabbit, the double cross simply for the picture of a black cross, but not to take the bare triangular figure for the picture of an object that has fallen over. To see this aspect of the triangle demands *imagination (Vorstellungskraft)*."[21] But later still he says something more general about seeing aspects. "The concept of as aspect is akin to the concept of an image. In other words: the concept 'I am now seeing it as . . .' is akin to 'I am now having *this* image.' "[22] Immediately afterwards he says: "Doesn't it take imagination *(Phantasie)* to hear something as a variation on a particular theme? And yet one is perceiving something in so hearing it."[23] Again on this page he says generally that seeing an aspect and imagining are alike subject to the will.

It is clear that in these references to imagination and to images Wittgenstein is doing at least two things. On the one hand he is *contrasting* the seeing of certain aspects with the seeing of others, and saying *of some only* that they require imagination; and, further, that some of these are cases in which an image is, as it were, in contact with the visual impression. On the other hand he is saying that there is a *general* kinship between the seeing of aspects and the having of images; though the only respect of kinship he mentions is that both are subject to the will. Perhaps we can make something of both of these.

As regards the first thing he is doing, the contrast he is making, cannot we find an analogy here with a whole host of situations in which there is some sort of departure from the imme-

20. Wittgenstein, p. 207.

21. Loc. cit.

22. Wittgenstein, p. 213.

23. Loc. cit.

diately obvious or familiar or mundane or established or super-
ficial or literal way of taking things; situations in which there is
some sort of innovation or extravagance or figure or trope or
stretch of the mind or new illumination or invention? Thus, beginning from such simplicities as seeing a cloud as a camel or a
formation of stalagmites as a dragon, or a small child at a picnic
seeing a tree stump as a table, we may move on to very diverse
things: to the first application of the word 'astringent' to a remark
or to someone's personality; to Wellington at Salamanca saying
"Now we have them" and seeing the future course of the battle
in an injudicious movement of the enemy; to the sensitive observer of a personal situation seeing that situation as one of
humiliation for one party and triumph for another; to a natural
(or even a social) scientist seeing a pattern in phenomena which
has never been seen before and introducing, as we say, new concepts to express his insight; to anyone seeing Keble College, Oxford, or the University Museum or Balliol Chapel as their architects
meant them to be seen; to Blake seeing eternity in a grain of
sand and heaven in a wild flower. And so on. In connection with
any item in this rather wild list the words 'imaginative' and
'imagination' are appropriate, though only to some of them is
the idea of an image coming into contact with an impression appropriate. But we must remember that what is obvious and
familiar, and what is not, is, at least to a large extent, a matter of
training and experience and cultural background. So it may be,
in this sense, imaginative of Eliot to see the river as a strong,
brown god, but less so of the members of a tribe who believe in
river-gods. It may, in this sense, call for imagination on my
part to see or hear something as a variation on a particular theme,
but not on the part of a historian of architecture or a trained
musician. What is fairly called exercise of imagination for one
person or age group or generation or society may be merest
routine for another. To say this is not, of course, in any way to
question the propriety of using the term 'imagination' to mark
a *contrast*, in any particular case, with routine perception in the
application of a concept. It is simply to draw attention to the

kind, or kinds, of contrast that are in question and in doing so to stress resemblances and *continuities* between contrasted cases. It should not take much effort to see the resemblances and continuities as at least as striking as the differences and so to sympathise with that imaginative employment of the term 'imagination' which leads both Hume and Kant to cast the faculty for the role of chief agent in the exercise of the power of concept-application, in general, over a variety of cases; to see why Hume described it as a "magical faculty" which is "most perfect in the greatest geniuses" and is "properly what we call a genius."

So we find a continuity between one aspect of Wittgenstein's use of the term and one aspect of Hume's and Kant's. What of the other aspect of Wittgenstein's use, where he finds a kinship, in *all* cases, between seeing an aspect and having an image? Well, let us consider the character of Wittgenstein's examples. Some are examples of what might be called essentially ambiguous figures, like the duck-rabbit or the double cross. Others are, as it were, very thin and schematic, like the cube-picture or the triangle. If we attend to the essentially ambiguous figures, it is clear that imagination in the sense just discussed would not normally be said to be required in order to see either aspect of either. Both aspects of each are entirely natural and routine, only they compete with each other in a way which is not usual in the case of ordinary objects. We can switch more or less easily from one aspect to another as we cannot normally do with ordinary objects of perception. But we might sometimes switch with similar ease in what on the face of it are ordinary cases: thus, standing at the right distance from my yellow flowering bush, I can switch from seeing it as such to seeing it as yellow chalk marks scrawled on the wall. So if the affinity between seeing aspects and having images is simply a matter of subjection to the will, and if subjection to the will is thought of in this way as ease of switching, then the affinity is present in this case as in the case of the visually ambiguous figures.

But is the general affinity between seeing aspects and having images simply a matter of subjection to the will? One may point out that the subjection of *seeing as* to the will is by no means absolute or universal. And it may be replied that the same is true of having images. One may be haunted or tortured by images, whether of recall or foreboding, from which one vainly seeks distraction but cannot dismiss, or escape the return of, if dismissed; or, alternatively, one may fail to picture something in one's mind when one tries.[24] So at least a *parallel* between *seeing as* and having images, in respect of subjection to the will, continues to hold.

But surely one may ask whether there is not a deeper affinity between *seeing as* and having an image, one which goes beyond this matter of subjection to the will, and can be found in general between perception and imaging. And surely there is. It has already been expressed in saying that the thought (or, as Kant might prefer, the concept) is alive in the perception just as it is in the image. The thought of something as an x or as a particular x is alive in the perception of it as an x or as a particular x just as the thought of an x or a particular x is alive in the having of an image of an x or a particular x. This is what is now sometimes expressed in speaking of the *intentionality* of perception, as of imaging.[25] But the idea is older than *this* application of that terminology, for the idea is in Kant.

Of course it is essential to the affinity that the having of an image, like perceiving, is more than just having a thought; and that the more that it is is what justifies us in speaking of an image as an actual representative of a nonactual perception and justifies Hume (for all the danger of it) in speaking of images as faint copies of impressions. As for the differences between them both in intrinsic character and in external, causal relations, there is perhaps no need to stress them here.

24. See p. 53 of Miss Ishiguro's admirable treatment of the whole subject in "Imagination," *Proceedings of Aristotelian Society,* Supp. Vol. 41 (1967).

25. See Miss Anscombe's "The Intentionality of Sensation: A Grammatical Feature" in *Analytical Philosophy, Second Series,* ed. R. J. Butler (Oxford, 1965), pp. 155–180.

VII

I began this paper by mentioning three areas of association in which the term 'imagination' and its cognates find employment: in connection with *images,* in connection with *innovation* or *invention,* and in connection with *mistakes,* including perceptual mistakes. I have referred to the first two areas of use, but not, so far, to the last. But perhaps it is worth glancing briefly at the quite common use of 'imagine' and 'imagination' in connection with the *seeing as* of perceptual mistakes. Suppose that when I see the yellow flowering bush as yellow chalk marks on the wall, I actually take what I see *to be* yellow chalk marks on the wall—as I may well do once, though probably not when I have the experience again. In such a case, as opposed to that of *seeing as* without *taking as,* it would be natural and correct to say: 'For a moment I imagined what I saw to be yellow chalk marks on the wall; then I looked again and saw it was a yellow flowering bush against the wall.'

Now it would be easy, and reasonable, to explain this 'mistake' use of 'imagine' by taking some other use or uses as primary and representing this use as an extension of it or them in such a way as to allow no role for imagination in ordinary routine perception.[26] But we should consider how it would be possible to give a kind of caricature-explanation on different lines. Of course, the explanation would run, this indispensable faculty of imagination is involved in ordinary routine perception. It is just that it would be highly misleading to single it out for mention as responsible for the outcome in the case of ordinary routine perception. For to do so would be to suggest that things are not as they normally are in ordinary routine perception. Thus we single the faculty out for mention when it operates without anything like the normal sensory stimulus altogether, as in imaging, delivering mental products unmistakably different from those

26. As, for example, by saying that when what presents itself as a perception (or memory) turns out to be erroneous, we *reclassify* it by assigning it to that faculty of which the essential role is, say, unfettered invention; somewhat as we sometimes refer to falsehood as *fiction.*

of ordinary perceptions; when, in one or another of many possible ways, it deviates from, or adds to, the response which we have come to consider routine; or when, as in the present case, we actually mistake the character of the source of stimulus. But it is absurd to conclude that because we only *name* the faculty in these cases, the faculty we then name is only operative in these cases. We might as well say that the faculty of verbalizing or uttering words is not exercised in intelligent conversation on the ground that we generally say things like 'He was verbalizing freely' or 'He uttered a lot of words' only when, for example, we mean that there was no sense or point in what he said.

It is not my purpose to represent such a line of argument as correct.[27] Still less am I concerned—even if I could do so—to elaborate or defend any account of what we really mean, or ought to mean, by 'imagination,' such as that line of argument might point to. I am not sure that either the question, what we *really* do *mean* by the word, or the question, what we *ought* to mean by it, are quite the right ones to ask in this particular case. What matters is that we should have a just sense of the very various and subtle connections, continuities and affinities, as well as differences, which exist in this area. The affinities between the image-having power and the power of ordinary perceptual recognition; the continuities between inventive or extended or playful concept-application and ordinary concept-application in perception: these are some things of which we may have a juster sense as a result of reflection on Kant's use of the term 'imagination'; even, in the latter case, as a result of reflection upon Hume's use of the term. A perspicuous and thorough survey of the area is, as far as I know, something that does not exist; though Wittgenstein's pages contain an intentionally unsystematic assemblage of some materials for such a survey.

27. It would be, it will be seen, an application (or misapplication) of a principle due to H. P. Grice. See "The Causal Theory of Perception," *Proceedings of Aristotelian Society*, Supp. Vol. 35 (1961), pp. 121–168.

Wilfrid Sellars
Toward a Theory of the Categories

I

Kant is clearly not an "empiricist," yet the concept of experience is central to his philosophy. This dissociation of the terms 'empiricism' and 'experience' is an interesting feature of how they have come to be used, not only in the Kantian tradition, but also, for example, in the pragmatic tradition according to John Dewey. The latter, as is well known, equated 'empiricism' with the 'atomistic' sensationalism of Hume and Mill, but used the term 'experience' in the spirit of German idealism and made it the central concept of his naturalistic pragmatism.

Philosophical 'isms' are as difficult to define as their political counterparts, and 'empiricism' is no exception, yet paradigm cases are presented by Hume, Mill and, more recently, by logical positivism. The Wittgenstein of the *Tractatus* is a particularly interesting case, because although he is clearly, in some respects, in the Humean tradition, he nevertheless conceives of the task of philosophy as that of giving an a priori account of what it is to be an object of empirical knowledge. In this respect he belongs in the tradition of Kant, for whom, as far as theoretical reason is concerned, the task of philosophy is exactly that of explicating the concept of an object of experience. Kant emphasizes that this task does not belong to empirical psychology; like Wittgenstein he conceives of it as a nonempirical enterprise. In effect he is convinced that it is possible to delineate the essential features of anything that could count as an object of empirical knowledge in any possible world, that is, for any finite mind, however different the world it inhabits might be from ours in its generic traits. Notice that these differences between possible worlds would concern not just their histories, but the very qualities, relations, and nomological connections which characterize the objects which make it up. In other words, Kant aimed at delineating the conceptual structure of the most generic features of the concept of an object of experience. Needless to say, however, he was also concerned to understand how these most generic features take specific form to constitute the concept of an object of *human* experience.

If we can say, as I think we can, that the *pure* categories are essential moments in the definition of an object of experience in general, then *schemata* are to be construed as the *differentia* which specify these generic moments into the specific categories of a variety of finite mind in its possible world; and the 'schematized categories' described by Kant become the categories involved in the explication of the concept of *human* experience, or, roughly, the experience of those finite centers of experience which share Space and, particularly, Time as forms of intuition. For, as Kant sees it, the distinctive feature of human experience is that it is experience of a world of spatiotemporal objects. In evaluating this conception, it must be remembered that Kant equates Space and Time with Newtonian Space and Time, and that he would grant that a world of experience might have a structure which, though not in this sense 'spatial' or 'temporal,' has properties which are analogous to the latter in ways which make possible a schematizing of the pure categories and hence which satisfy the abstract requirements of a concept of a world of experience which has been purified of all contingent features.

The points I have been making so far can be summed up in the following statement. Both Kant and Wittgenstein think it possible to give an a priori account of what it is to be an object of empirical knowledge. Obviously the accounts they give differ in interesting ways—ways which reflect the different conceptual resources on which they could draw. For the intervening century saw two intellectual revolutions which have already wrought irreversible changes in the philosopher's environment. Of these revolutions the most important was the impact of evolutionary theory on what are now called "The Life Sciences."

Less important, but by no means insignificant—though its significance has been exaggerated—was the revolution in logical theory which triumphed with the *Principia Mathematica* of Whitehead and Russell; for both Kant and Wittgenstein took as their point of departure in explicating the concept of an object of empirical knowledge, the forms and operations in terms of which the logical theory of their time interpreted the structure of statements and the validity of inferences.

II

I have pointed out that Kant believed it possible to explicate the concept of an object of empirical knowledge in a way which abstracts from the specifics of human experience. I shall now proceed to argue that the same is true of the Wittgenstein of the *Tractatus*. To begin with, it is a familiar and tantalizing fact that he gives an account of *objects*, not only without giving any examples, but without even indicating what sort of examples it would be appropriate to give. Thus, whereas Kant does tie his abstract account to distinctive features of human experience, Wittgenstein makes no such concession and does indeed give an account of what it is to be an object *überhaupt*.

Many contemporary philosophers think of themselves as belonging to the 'empiricist tradition,' and yet are increasingly attracted to those features of Kant's thought which are not peripheral to but, indeed, central to his clash with 'empiricism.' It is, I would argue, no mere coincidence that this phenomenon has been accompanied by a revival of interest in the *Tractatus* and a growing awareness of the extent to which it diverges from classical empiricism and is profoundly Kantian in character.

Are we to interpret this trend as an absorption of Kantian themes into empiricism or as a reinterpretation of Kantian themes along empiricist lines? These questions call for decisions rather than answers. Which gives us more insight: a contrast between empiricised Kant and historical Kant; or a contrast between Kantanised empiricism and historical empiricism? One thing is clear. The traditions are merging and neither will ever again be the same.

III

I pointed out that for Kant, the explication of the concept of an object of empirical knowledge requires a theory of 'categories.' The same is no less true of Wittgenstein, and, indeed, I have been implying that their treatment of 'categories' is importantly similar. Yet on what principle do philosophers collect certain concepts together and label them 'categories'? For offering a theory of categories presupposes that one has such a principle of collection in mind. Historically, the principle has evolved with the theory. The initial clumsiness with which it was formulated reflected the inadequacies of early theory. Indeed, the sophistication of the principle of collection is just the sophistication of the theory. The initial move toward a collection of and a theory of categories is to be found in Plato's *Sophist.* The approach is a subtle one. Indeed as in the case of so many other aspects of Plato's thought, it achieved a degree of insight which was not soon to be equalled. Yet its explication would require an elaborate scholarly apparatus, and in a paper to fit the allotted space, two is company and three a crowd. On the other hand, a reference to the Aristotelian tradition is indispensable, though when Aristotle characterizes the categories as 'highest kinds' (*summa genera*) of entity he is building, as usual, on Platonic ground. It is this conception of the categories which is one of the abiding themes, if not *the* abiding theme, of traditional *Kategorienlehre.*

To approach the conception of categories as *summa genera* in terms of what have been traditionally regarded as paradigmatic examples—thus, substance, quality, and relation—is to embark on a sea of perplexity. What would it be to construe *substance* as a *summum genus?* The natural temptation is to think of such a series of classificatory statements as

Fido is a dachshund
Fido is a dog
Fido is a brute
Fido is an animal

Fido is a corporeal substance
Fido is a substance.

Parity of reasoning would lead us, in the case of quality, to some such sequence as

x is a red
x is a color
x is a perceptual quality
x is a quality,

for if we tried

x is red
x is colored
⋮

it would be necessary at some stage to make a radical change in syntax in order to end up with

x is a quality.

On the other hand, if we stick with

x is a red,

what sort of item could x be? One answer trips readily off the tongue: x is an abstract entity, a universal. On the other hand, we can appeal to the familiar, but heterodox idea of what have been called 'particularized qualities,' or 'qualitative particulars.' Actually we have no choice, as we soon discover if we attempt to apply the second strategy to the case of relations. Only a series of even more desperate moves can keep us from falling immediately into the obvious absurdities exploited by Bradley.[1] We are, therefore, committed to the former alternative, that is that what belongs in the place of 'x' is an expression which refers to an abstract entity. Our search for *summa genera* leads us to the sequences

1. I have discussed some of these expedients in "Meditations Leibnitziennes," *American Philosophical Quarterly*, ii (1965), reprinted in my *Philosophical Perspectives* (Springfield, Illinois, 1967).

Red(ness)[2] is a color
Red(ness) is a perceptible quality
Red(ness) is a quality,

and

Juxtaposition is a spatial relation
Juxtaposition is a dyadic relation
Juxtaposition is a relation.

But if the entities which belong to the categories of quality and relation are *universals,* then to assert that there are qualities would seem to be to make an 'ontological commitment' to abstract entities.

Now I take it as obvious that there are, in some sense of 'are,' qualities and relations. So I take it as obvious that there are, in some sense of 'are,' universals, and, in general, abstract entities. Yet is it so clear that the statements

There are qualities
There are relations

make an 'ontological commitment'? Or is it possible for a philosopher consistently to assert

There are qualities

but add, in a different philosophical tone of voice, there *really* are no such things as qualities and relations? I shall pick up this theme shortly.

IV

The empiricist tradition had little light to throw on categorial concepts. Much of what they had to say can be regarded as a *reductio ad absurdum* of the principle: *nihil in intellectu quod non fuit prius*

---

2. Color words are notoriously ambiguous in the sense that they function sometimes as adjectives, sometimes as singular terms (as above), sometimes as common nouns (for example in 'crimson is a shade of red').

in sensu. Roughly this principle tells us that, in the case of simple and most specific concepts, expressions which belong in the context

concept of *x*

must also belong in the context

impression of *x*.

Obviously, the more limited the scope of the latter context, the more limited the scope of the former. At the hands of Hume the principle led to a rejection of the traditional interpretation of substance as a simple idea. Yet even in his reinterpretation of substance it remains a *summum genus,* and, in general, the Aristotelean conception of categories as *summa genera* and, hence, of categorial concepts as most generic concepts, lingered on, though particular categories were pruned or reconstrued. Thus Hume's intriguing account of generic ideas was intended to apply not only, for example, to the generic idea of triangularity, but also to such philosophically interesting ideas as those of substance, quality, relation, unity and even, it would seem, existence.

It is not my purpose in this essay to criticize radical concept empiricism. It is so vulnerable, indeed, that it is no easy task to relocate its insights in a correct account of the conceptual order. One would expect that, properly understood, it would turn out to be true a priori, like the theory of categories. Historically, of course, empiricists have never been clear as to the status of their fundamental principles. Are they, perhaps, appeals to Ockham's razor? Or are they sweeping generalizations?

Another feature of the empiricist tradition is its 'logical atomism,' according to which every basic piece of empirical knowledge is logically independent of every other. Notice that this independence concerns not only *what* is known, but the *knowing* of it. The second dimension of this 'atomism' is of particular importance for understanding Kant's rejection of empiricism, although its relation to his theory of categories has not always been clearly understood. That the Wittgenstein of the *Tractatus* agrees with Kant in rejecting this dimension of the 'logical atomism' of the empiricist tradition—not without raising unanswered questions about what is to count as a *logical* connection[3]—is equally relevant to *his* theory of categories. But this, also, is a topic for which preparation must be made.

V

The first major breakthrough in the theory of categories came, as one might expect, in the late Middle Ages, when logic, like knighthood, was in flower. A new strategy was developed for coping with certain puzzling concepts which were the common concern of logicians and metaphysicians. This strategy is illustrated by Ockham's explication of such statements as

A) Man is a species.

Roughly, he construes it to have the sense of

B) 'Man' is a sortal mental term,

where, since mental terms are to be conceived as analogous to linguistic expressions in overt speech, the quotation marks are designed to make it clear that in statement (A) we are *mentioning* a concept rather than *using* it, as we would be if we were to judge that Tom is a man.

To this we must add, I believe, that whereas in (B) the expression ''Man'' presents itself as a name, it need not, and should not, be so construed. Its 'depth grammar' places it in quite a different box. A parallel will, perhaps, be helpful. Consider the statement

c) 'And' is a logical expression.

It is clear that although the grammatical subject of this statement is a *singular term*, it need not be construed as a *name*. For, clearly, to talk about 'and' is to talk about occurrences of 'and,' (that is 'and's). We might, therefore, be tempted to say that in this context

3. Is 'transcendental logic' just another *application* of 'ordinary logic'?

" 'and' " is functioning as a *general term*. Taken seriously, however, this suggestion would require us to reformulate (c) as

c_1) 'And's are logical expressions.

But, then, we remember the 'institutional' use of 'the' and see that we can have our cake and eat it too. For we can interpret our original statement (c) to have the form

c_2) (The) 'and' is a logical expression,

which is the equivalent of

c_3) 'And's are logical expressions,

in the sense in which 'The lion is tawny' is equivalent to 'lions are tawny.'

If, now, we take seriously the concept of thinkings as 'inner speech' (Plato's 'dialogue within the soul'), then Ockham's analysis of

Man is a species,

when developed along the lines just indicated, would construe (B) as

B_1) The 'man' is a sortal mental term

and, hence, as equivalent to

B_2) 'Man's are sortal terms.

Notice that although, according to this account, the original statement (A) is to be construed as referring to conceptual items, so that, *in a sense*, the expression 'man' in this context is equivalent to the expression 'the 'man',' it would be a mistake to rewrite the original statement to read

A_1) The 'man' is a species,

for the context

——is a species

already does the quoting, so that (A_1) is, according to the analysis, to be construed as

A₂) The ˙the˙man˙˙ is a mental sortal term

that is

A₃) ˙The˙man˙˙s are mental sortal terms

which is, however, false, since ˙the ˙man˙˙s are mental singular terms. Thus if we introduce the phrase 'distributive singular term' for expressions formed by prefixing the institutional 'the' to a sortal expression, for example 'the lion,' then ˙the ˙man˙˙s would be mental distributive singular terms.

Exactly the same point must be made about the statement

D) Socrates is a substance, that is a primary individual.

By parity of reasoning it would have, using the above strategy, the form

D₁) ˙Socrates˙ is a basic mental singular term,

in other words,

D₂) The ˙Socrates˙ is a basic mental singular term,

or, again,

D₃) ˙Socrates˙s are basic mental singular terms.[4]

Here, again, it would be a mistake to assume that if (D) is, in a sense, about conceptual items, that is ˙Socrates˙s, then it would be legitimate to rewrite it as

D₄) The ˙Socrates˙ is a substance, that is a primary individual.

For according to the analysis, this would be equivalent in sense to

˙The ˙Socrates˙˙ is a basic mental singular term,

that is

˙The ˙Socrates˙˙s are basic mental singular terms.

4. Examples of singular terms which are *not* basic would be, for example, 'the average man,' 'the tallest building in Manhattan,' 'the lion,' and 'Jack and Jill' as in 'Jack and Jill is a team.' (Of course in ordinary English we would say 'Jack and Jill are a team,' but then it is quite clear that the 'are' is not functioning as it would in 'Jack and Jill are children,' which simply abbreviates 'Jack is a child and Jill is a child.')

But the latter are false, for although 'the 'Socrates''s *are* singular terms, they are not *basic* singular terms, but rather distributive singular terms, and, as such, to be classified with defined expressions. Thus, according to the above analysis, mental assertions or judgments with

'The 'Socrates''s

as their subjects are dispensable in favor of statements with

''Socrates''s

as their subject, just as, in overt speech, statements with

'The pawn's

as their subject, for example

The pawn is a chess piece

are dispensable in favor of statements with

'pawns'

as their subject, for example

Pawns are chess pieces.

What all this amounts to is that to apply Ockham's strategy to the theory of categories is to construe categories as classifications of conceptual items. This becomes, in Kant's hands, the idea that categories are the most generic functional classifications of the elements of judgments.

One might put this by saying that instead of being *summa genera* of entities which are objects 'in the world,' a notion which, as we saw, would force us to construe qualities, relations, and so forth as empirical objects, categories are *summa genera* of conceptual items. But while this is, I believe, the correct move to make, it raises the further question—what is the sense of 'in the world' which applies to 'empirical objects' but not to conceptual items? Indeed, *in the world* seems to be another category which, if we are to be consistent, must itself be construed as applying to conceptual items.

Assuming, however, that this apparent difficulty can be met, let us watch the theory grow. In the first place, once we take this general line, we see that we might be able to distinguish between 'formal' and 'material' categories. For just as it is plausible to say that

Quality is a *summum genus* of entity,

so it seems proper to say that

Color is a *summum genus* of perceptual quality.

This suggests that an adequate theory of categories would involve a distinction between 'determinables' and 'determinates.'

In the second place the theory suggests that in addition to such standard examples as 'substance,' 'quality,' 'relation,' and so forth, this list of categories should be expanded to include not only the 'modalities' but also 'state of affairs' as a 'formal' category, with 'event' and, perhaps, 'action' as 'material' categories subsumed under it.[5]

In the third place it is to be noted that implicit in the above account of categories is a theory of abstract entities. For if

Man is a species

is tantamount to

The ˙man˙ is a sortal conceptual item,

then we are committed to the idea that statements about the abstract entity *man* are dispensible in favor of statements about conceptual items, that is those acts and dispositions which involve 'predicates' to which the general term

˙man˙

would apply.

Of course, there is always the temptation to say that to be a mental term of the sort to which the general term "man"

5. It is worth noting at this point that 'species' as a classification of conceptual items would not be a category in the sense of *summum genus*, for it falls under the more generic notion of 'character.' For both 'man' and 'animal,' not to mention 'white,' are ways of characterizing individual things.

applies is to be a mental term which stands for the abstract entity *man,* or the character *being human.* But the above approach can be generalized into the idea that *every* use of abstract singular terms is essentially classificatory, a matter of classifying conceptual items. Thus, to return to the linguistic level,

'Gelb' (in G) means yellow,

and its more regimented counterpart

'Gelb' (in G) stands for yellowness,

can be construed as classifying *'gelb's* (in G) as yellow's, that is as doing in German the job done in our language by the predicate 'yellow.'

If so, then

Yellow (yellowness) is a quality

would have the sense of

The 'yellow' is a (one-place) predicate (in mentalese),

and 'reduce' to

'Yellow's are predicates,

where to be a 'yellow' is to be an item having a certain conceptual job, which would ultimately be explained in terms of the word-word and word-world uniformities by virtue of which 'yellow's in one language and *'gelb's* in German function as they do in basic matter-of-factual statements.[6]

In the fourth place, while the theory permits us to say

Yellow is an entity,

6. Note that linguistic items proper—and not just 'inner speech' episodes—are now being treated as conceptual items. For a defense of the thesis that overt verbal behavior—which is the primary mode of being of the linguistic proper—is *as such* conceptual in character, see my "Language as Thought and as Communication," *Philosophy and Phenomenological Research,* XXIX (1969), pp. 506–527. For an exploration of the relation between the concept of thought as 'inner speech' and the concept of thinking-out-loud (candid overt speech) see my *Science and Metaphysics* (New York, 1968), chap. III.

ascribing to this, roughly, the sense of

The 'yellow' is a meaningful mentalese term,

it must deny

Yellow is an individual,

for the latter would have the sense of

The 'yellow' is a mentalese singular term,

which is false. In other words, 'Yellow is a primary entity' might be true, but not 'Yellow is a primary individual.' It would, therefore, be correct to say that *there are entities which are not individuals,* an ostensibly paradoxical statement which, nevertheless, many perceptive philosophers have been led by intuitive, if not always perspicuous, considerations to make.

Finally, notice that the theory would enable us to explain how a philosopher could be justified in acknowledging that

There are qualities, for example triangularity

while denying that there *really* are qualities. For such statements about qualities as have the form

The 'triangular' is . . .

can be paraphrased without the use of a singular term. Might one not acknowledge that there are chess pieces, for example the pawn, while denying that there *really* are chess pieces, for example the pawn? Thus a respectable and philosophically important sense could be given to the claim that although there *really are* particular conceptual episodes of thinking that something is triangular, there *really* is no such entity as the quality of being triangular.

VI

To appreciate the distinctive features of Kant's 'metaphysics of experience,' it is helpful to approach it *via* the early Wittgenstein, although this might seem an attempt to illuminate the obscure through the more obscure. For, contrary to the usual conception, Wittgenstein's views are actually as clear and straightforward as he thought them to be.[7]

Wittgenstein conceives of basic empirical truths as consisting of expressions referring to simple objects and predicates which stand for simple matter-of-factual qualities and relations. Expressions for complex individuals and complex characters can in principle be eliminated in favor of these 'elementary' expressions. Wittgenstein does not deny, as is often thought, that expressions which do not occur in basic statements (or are not definable in terms of them) can be meaningful. He simply denies that they refer to or describe objects *in the world*. Their meaningfulness may consist in the fact that they enable us to formulate truths about *our thoughts about* objects in the world. One must also carefully distinguish between the way in which logical connectives are meaningful, although they do not refer to or characterize objects in the world, from that in which such meta-conceptual terms as 'object,' 'quality,' and 'fact' are meaningful.

This philosophical denial of existence to complex individuals and characters underlies Wittgenstein's claim that it is an essential feature of the objects of empirical knowledge that they be simple and have simple matter-of-factual characters. Another essential feature is that these objects be the referents of a referring expression in the living language (and of the corresponding mental terms) of those for whom they are objects. Yet just as simplicity and individuality are not attributes of objects, although objects are simple individuals, so *being the referent* of a referring expression is not a *relation* between an object and the expression.

This feature of Wittgenstein's thought has seemed to many to be a most intolerable paradox, for the following two statements are obviously true:

A) The objects of empirical knowledge include referring expressions as linguistic or mentalese tokens (tokenings).

7. That it was not easy to appreciate this at the time is but one more illustration of the fact that the more intelligible in the order of being does not always coincide with the more intelligible in the order of knowing.

B) Referring expressions would not refer to objects unless they stood in matter-of-factual relations to objects.

It is only too tempting to conclude from the truth of (A) and (B) that *reference* is a matter-of-factual relation, and hence that the character of referring to an object is a matter-of-factual relational property. Surely, if

C) Expression E denotes something

entails

C') Expression E stands in matter-of-factual relations to something

and

D) Expression E denotes something

entails

D') There is something, for example Socrates, to which E refers

then

E refers to Socrates

must have the form

R(E, Socrates).

But this would be a mistake, as can be seen from certain parallels. Consider

'Oder' (in G) stands for something,

that is

There is something for which 'oder' (in G) stands, that is disjunction.

Clearly this entails that certain empirical facts hold of 'oder' in German. Yet it would be implausible to suggest that *standing for* is an empirical relation between the German word 'oder' and disjunction, or alternation or, to simplify the point, or-ness.

For, according to our strategy, to say what 'oder' specifically means or stands for is to classify 'oder's (in German) as 'or's.

And it is by virtue of being 'or's, and not by virtue of standing in a supposed empirical relation of *standing for*, that certain empirical facts must be true of *'oder's*.

Consider another parallel:

(In our games of chess) tall cones play (serve as) bishops.

Clearly in order for tall cones to play the bishop, certain empirical truths must hold of tall cones (in the relevant contexts). But it is the criteria for *being a bishop* which carry these empirical requirements, not the supposed relation of *playing* or *serving as*. Indeed

Tall cones play (serve as) the bishop

can be paraphrased as

Tall cones *are* bishops,

and, obviously, 'are' is not a word for an empirical relation.[8]

One who is half convinced might say that this is all very well and good with respect to the context

—— stands for . . .

but does it throw light on 'denotes'? And, indeed, 'denotes,' or 'refers to,' unlike 'stands for' or its Fregean counterpart 'expresses,' is no mere specialized version of the copula. But one can grant this without granting that reference or denotation is an empirical relation.

Consider the contrast between

'Centaur' (in ε) denotes (or refers to) nothing,

and

'Centaur' (in ε) stands for the property of being a Centaur.

The former differs from the latter not by saying that 'centaur' fails to stand in a certain empirical relation to anything, but by telling us that the kind—left open—for which 'centaur' stands is

8. It is philosophically of the utmost importance that 'men are animals' when translated into PMese becomes 'man⊂animal' which is short for '(x) (x is a man ⊃ x is an animal).' In this sense 'are' dissolves into connectives (not relations) and quantification.

empty, that is, is not exemplified by or true of anything. Again,

'Man' (in ε) denotes featherless biped

differs from

'Man' (in ε) stands for rational animal

not by doing the radically different job of telling us that certain items stand in an empirical relation, but by telling us that the kind—left open—for which 'man' stands is exemplified by or true of all and only those items which also exemplify the character of being a featherless biped.

The same general account can be given of the denotation of singular terms, though the details must be left for *another* occasion.[9] Thus

'Parigi' (in Italian) denotes the capital of France

would be construed as

'Parigi' (in Italian) stands for a concept which is materially equivalent to the concept ˙the capital of France˙.

Accordingly, although

'Parigi' (in Italian) denotes something

would entail that the word 'Parigi' (in Italian) stands in empirical relations, these relations would not *constitute* a relation of denoting but would serve as criteria for the classification which is left unspecified by the statement. The cash for such denotation statements would be of the form

'Parigi' (in Italian) stands for the ˙Paris˙ and the

˙Paris˙ is materially equivalent to the ˙the capital of France˙,

which imparts the information that 'Parigi's (in Italian) are ˙Paris˙s, and hence satisfy the criteria associated with this classification.

I conclude that Wittgenstein was right in claiming that *reference* is not a matter-of-factual relation, although the fact that a term refers entails that it stands in certain matter-of-factual rela-

9. See *Science and Metaphysics*, chap. III.

tions. That it stand, at least contingently, in such and such matter-of-factual relations to objects in the world is known by knowing its *reference*. Those in which it *necessarily* stands can only be determined by tracing out the implications of its *sense*, that is what it stands for.

Parallel points can be made with respect to predicates. Thus, for *'dreieckig'*s (in G) to stand for triangularity it must be true that they are caught up in certain word-word and word-thing uniformities. No more than in the other cases, however, do the latter constitute a supposed empirical relation of *standing for*.

VII

We can now turn our attention to the fact that for something to be an object of empirical knowledge, statements about it must be verifiable. There must, that is, be a method or strategy for deciding whether it is true or false. Here, again, the correct account has an initial appearance of paradox. Surely, to determine that a statement is true is to determine that it corresponds to a fact. Yet facts are not objects, and on Tractarian principles only objects can have matter-of-factual attributes and stand in matter-of-factual relations.

On the other hand, it is presumably a contingent or matter-of-factual fact that a given statement is true. How can we render consistent the ideas that (a) facts are not objects; (b) only objects can stand in matter-of-factual relations; (c) the truth of a statement is a matter-of-factual relation between the statement and a fact? Are not true statements those which correspond to facts?

The above treatment of *categories, standing for,* and *denotation* suggests the way out. According to it

'*a* is ϕ' (in L) corresponds to (the fact) that *a* is ϕ

no more *asserts* that '*a* is ϕ' (in L) stands in a matter-of-factual relation to something in the world than

E denotes O

asserts that ε and something in the world stand in a matter-of-factual relation of denotation. 'That *a* is φ' is to be construed as a distributive singular term ('the ˙*a* is φ˙') which, like 'the ˙triangular˙,' applies to conceptual items. Again, 'that *a* is φ is a fact' is to be construed, in first approximation, as having the sense of 'the ˙*a* is φ˙ is correctly[10] assertible.' Thus the original statement does two things: (a) it classifies ˙*a* is φ's (in L) as ˙*a* is φ˙s; (b) it tells us that the latter, which according to (a) include ˙*a* is φ's (in L), are correctly assertible.

On the other hand, just as

ε denotes ο,

though it does not *assert* a matter-of-factual relation to obtain between ε and ο, nevertheless entails that ε stands in a complex empirical relationship to ο, so

'*a* is φ' (in L) corresponds to the fact that *a* is φ,

while it does not *assert* that a relation obtains between '*a* is φ' and the fact, nevertheless entails that certain matter-of-factual relations hold between '*a* is φ's as belonging to L, and the object *a*— *not* the fact that *a* is φ. It entails, that is, that '*a* is φ's as conceptual objects stand in certain complex empirical relationships to other objects. *Which* objects is determined by the *empirical relationships* which must be satisfied if 'φ' is to stand (in L) for a certain characteristic and '*a*' is to denote (in L) a certain object.

Thus the matter-of-factual characteristics of ˙*a* is φ's (in L) as conceptual objects which are entailed by their truth do not constitute a supposed relation of "correspondence to a fact." They are, rather, matter-of-factual relations to genuine objects. In the

10. The relevant correctnesses are those which "give meaning to expressions" and are to be distinguished from the correctnesses which concern the role of language in communication and personal interaction. For an elaboration of this point, see *Science and Metaphysics,* chap. iv; also "Language as Thought and as Communication," *Philosophy and Phenomenological Research,* xxix (1969), pp. 506–527.

case of basic empirical truths, on which the above account has been focused, these relations are different in each case, although they can all be subsumed under the general formula:

Tokens of 'x is f' (and 'xRy') as expressions (in L) (or in mentalese) have matter-of-factual characteristics by virtue of which they are linguistic projections—in accordance with certain semantical uniformities—of the objects to which these expressions refer.

We can sum this up as follows: In the case of basic empirical statements, unless the linguistic episodes which are their tokens stand in a projective relation to other objects in the world, they would not be true. On the other hand, to characterize these statements as true (that is as corresponding to facts) is not to specify the projective relation in question.

The above line of thought is reinforced by considerations pertaining to logical and mathematical truth. Thus it is a fact that $2 + 2 = 4$. And

'II + II = IV' (in L) corresponds to the fact that $2 + 2 = 4$

trips readily off the tongue. Yet it is implausible in the extreme to suppose that in this context 'corresponds' stands for a matter-of-factual relation between 'II + II = IV' (in L) and an extraconceptual entity. As before, 'corresponds to fact' dissolves into classification,

'II + II = IV's (in L) are '$2 + 2 = 4$'s,

and the ascription of correct assertibility to '$2 + 2 = 4$'s. This time, however, the relevant criteria of correctness are intralinguistic (or syntactical) and do not concern word-thing connections.

VIII

As the final step in this exploration of the concept of an object of empirical knowledge, I turn to considerations which were at the very center of Kant's thought,[11] but at best implicit in the *Tractatus,* lurking, if at all, in Kant's obscure dicta concerning the metaphysical 'I' and the status of the causal principle.

If empirical knowability is always knowability *by* a person *here* and *now,* whereas the *scope* of the knowable includes facts about the *there* and *then;* or if (to abstract from the specific conditions of human knowledge and move to the 'pure pragmatics' or 'transcendental logic' of empirical knowledge as such) knowability essentially involves a perspectival relationship between act of knowing and object known, must not the knowability of objects consist, in large part, of *inferential* knowability? (One can, of course, recognize the *essential* and *irreducible* role of inference without denying the existence of noninferential knowledge of the *here-now.*) On the other hand we have learned from Hume that facts about the *there* and *then* are never *logically* implied by facts about the *here* and *now,* but, at best, by the latter together with the general facts captured by true lawlike statements.

Now if we assume in the spirit of Hume that it is a contingent fact that such general facts obtain, it would seem to follow that it is a contingent fact that *there-then* objects are knowable. But if to be an object is to be a knowable, our conclusion would have to be that it is a contingent fact that there are *there-then* objects. But surely any *here-now* object is on its way *to* being a *there-then* object in the past and on its way *from* having been a *there-then* object in the future.

If so, then there would seem to be a *logical* inconsistency in granting the existence of *here-now* objects while denying that of *there-then* objects. A transcendental argument does not prove that there *is* empirical knowledge—what premises could such an argument have?—nor that there are *objects* of empirical knowledge. It simply explicates the concepts of *empirical knowledge* and *object of empirical knowledge.* Thus, to admit knowing that it *now* seems

11. For an elaboration of the points I am about to make which brings out their specifically Kantian character, see "Some Reflections on Kant's Theory of Experience," *The Journal of Philosophy,* LXIV (1967), pp. 633–647.

to me that there is a red and triangular object over there is to admit knowing that this *was about to* seem to me to be the case. If the skeptic (after making a similar move with respect to Space) attempts to replace the now of the seeming by the semblance of a now, by putting Time itself into the content of that which seems, does it not reappear (at least implicitly) outside this context—thus: *It (now) seems to me* that there is such a thing as Time (an order of before and after) in the *now* of which (and as Space in the *there* of which) there is a red and triangular object. (And does it merely seem to *me* that there is such a thing as I?)

What Kant takes himself to have proved is that the concept of empirical knowedge involves the concept of inferability in accordance with laws of nature. To grant that there is knowledge of the *here* and *now* is, he argues, to grant that there are general truths of the sort captured by lawlike statements. As far as specifically human knowledge is concerned, he was convinced that the idea that knowable objects are located in Space and Time carries with it certain general commitments as to the *form* of these laws. These commitments could, he thought, be known a priori or noninductively. Thus, the transcendental knowledge that spatiotemporal objects of knowledge must conform to certain generalizations *which are themselves logically synthetic* is itself, according to Kant, analytic.

Notice that the full expression of what is known in synthetic a priori knowledge has the form:

> Spatiotemporal knowables must conform to (synthetic) general truths satisfying such and such conditions.

That is:

> *If* there is knowledge of spatiotemporal objects, *then* these objects conform to general truths satisfying such and such conditions.

This statement as a whole is an analytic or explicative statement belonging to transcendental philosophy. If we are willing to affirm the antecedent—that is, if we are willing to grant, as even Hume does, that we do have knowledge of the *here* and *now*, then we can affirm the consequent, that is:

Spatiotemporal objects in my world conform to general truths satisfying such and such conditions.

It is, however, essential to note that the latter, *by itself*, is not a necessary truth, except in the derivative sense that it is necessary *relative to the antecedent.* To construe it as *intrinsically* necessary is to commit a modal fallacy of a piece with

Necessary (if all men are bipeds then all Texans are bipeds);
All men are bipeds;
So, necessary (all Texans are bipeds).

It is this conception of transcendental philosophy which distinguishes the critical rationalism of Kant (and the Wittgenstein of the *Tractatus*) from both dogmatic rationalism and the naive empiricism which thinks that empiricism is an empirical 'ism.'

Donald Davidson
Mental Events

MENTAL EVENTS such as perceivings, rememberings, decisions, and
actions resist capture in the nomological net of physical theory.[1]
How can this fact be reconciled with the causal role of mental
events in the physical world? Reconciling freedom with causal
determinism is a special case of the problem if we suppose that
causal determinism entails capture in, and freedom requires
escape from, the nomological net. But the broader issue can remain alive even for someone who believes a correct analysis of
free action reveals no conflict with determinism. *Autonomy* (freedom, self-rule) may or may not clash with determinism; *anomaly*
(failure to fall under a law) is, it would seem, another matter.

I start from the assumption that both the causal dependence,
and the anomalousness, of mental events are undeniable facts.
My aim is therefore to explain, in the face of apparent difficul-
ties, how this can be. I am in sympathy with Kant when he says,

> it is as impossible for the subtlest philosophy as for the
> commonest reasoning to argue freedom away. Philosophy
> must therefore assume that no true contradiction will be
> found between freedom and natural necessity in the same
> human actions, for it cannot give up the idea of nature
> any more than that of freedom. Hence even if we should
> never be able to conceive how freedom is possible, at
> least this apparent contradiction must be convincingly erad-
> icated. For if the thought of freedom contradicts itself or
> nature . . . it would have to be surrendered in competition
> with natural necessity.[2]

1. I was helped and influenced by Daniel Bennett, Sue Larson, and
Richard Rorty, who are not responsible for the result. My research was
supported by the National Science Foundation and the Center for Ad-
vanced Study in the Behavioral Sciences.

2. *Fundamental Principles of the Metaphysics of Morals,* trans. T. K. Abbott
(London, 1909), pp. 75-76.

Generalize human actions to mental events, substitute anomaly for freedom, and this is a description of my problem. And of course the connection is closer, since Kant believed freedom entails anomaly.

Now let me try to formulate a little more carefully the "apparent contradiction" about mental events that I want to discuss and finally dissipate. It may be seen as stemming from three principles.

The first principle asserts that at least some mental events interact causally with physical events. (We could call this the Principle of Causal Interaction.) Thus for example if someone sank the *Bismarck*, then various mental events such as perceivings, notings, calculations, judgments, decisions, intentional actions and changes of belief played a causal role in the sinking of the *Bismarck*. In particular, I would urge that the fact that someone sank the *Bismarck* entails that he moved his body in a way that was caused by mental events of certain sorts, and that this bodily movement in turn caused the *Bismarck* to sink.[3] Perception illustrates how causality may run from the physical to the mental: if a man perceives that a ship is approaching, then a ship approaching must have caused him to come to believe that a ship is approaching. (Nothing depends on accepting these as examples of causal interaction.)

Though perception and action provide the most obvious cases where mental and physical events interact causally, I think reasons could be given for the view that all mental events ultimately, perhaps through causal relations with other mental events, have causal intercourse with physical events. But if there are mental events that have no physical events as causes or effects, the argument will not touch them.

The second principle is that where there is causality, there

3. These claims are defended in my "Actions, Reasons and Causes," *The Journal of Philosophy*, LX (1963), pp. 685-700 and in "Agency," a paper forthcoming in the proceedings of the November, 1968, colloquium on Agent, Action, and Reason at the University of Western Ontario, London, Canada.

must be a law: events related as cause and effect fall under strict deterministic laws. (We may term this the Principle of the Nomological Character of Causality.) This principle, like the first, will be treated here as an assumption, though I shall say something by way of interpretation.[4]

The third principle is that there are no strict deterministic laws on the basis of which mental events can be predicted and explained (the Anomalism of the Mental).

The paradox I wish to discuss arises for someone who is inclined to accept these three assumptions or principles, and who thinks they are inconsistent with one another. The inconsistency is not, of course, formal unless more premises are added. Nevertheless it is natural to reason that the first two principles, that of causal interaction, and that of the nomological character of causality, together imply that at least some mental events can be predicted and explained on the basis of laws, while the principle of the anomalism of the mental denies this. Many philosophers have accepted, with or without argument, the view that the three principles do lead to a contradiction. It seems to me, however, that all three principles are true, so that what must be done is to explain away the appearance of contradiction; essentially the Kantian line.

The rest of this paper falls into three parts. The first part describes a version of the identity theory of the mental and the physical that shows how the three principles may be reconciled. The second part argues that there cannot be strict psychophysical laws; this is not quite the principle of the anomalism of the mental, but on reasonable assumptions entails it. The last part tries to show that from the fact that there can be no strict psychophysical laws, and our other two principles, we can infer the truth of a version of the identity theory, that is, a theory that identifies at least some mental events with physical events. It is clear that this

4. In "Causal Relations," *The Journal of Philosophy*, LXIV (1967), pp. 691–703, I elaborate on the view of causality assumed here. The stipulation that the laws be deterministic is stronger than required by the reasoning, and will be relaxed.

"proof" of the identity theory will be at best conditional, since two of its premises are unsupported, and the argument for the third may be found less than conclusive. But even someone unpersuaded of the truth of the premises may be interested to learn how they may be reconciled and that they serve to establish a version of the identity theory of the mental. Finally, if the argument is a good one, it should lay to rest the view, common to many friends and some foes of identity theories, that support for such theories can come only from the discovery of psychophysical laws.

I

The three principles will be shown consistent with one another by describing a view of the mental and the physical that contains no inner contradiction and that entails the three principles. According to this view, mental events are identical with physical events. Events are taken to be unrepeatable, dated individuals such as the particular eruption of a volcano, the (first) birth or death of a person, the playing of the 1968 World Series, or the historic utterance of the words, "You may fire when ready, Gridley." We can easily frame identity statements about individual events; examples (true or false) might be:

The death of Scott = the death of the author of *Waverley;*
The assassination of the Archduke Ferdinand = the event that started the First World War;
The eruption of Vesuvius in A.D. 79 = the cause of the destruction of Pompeii.

The theory under discussion is silent about processes, states, and attributes if these differ from individual events.

What does it mean to say that an event is mental or physical? One natural answer is that an event is physical if it is describable in a purely physical vocabulary, mental if describable in mental terms. But if this is taken to suggest that an event is physical, say, if some physical predicate is true of it, then there is the following difficulty. Assume that the predicate 'x took place at Noosa Heads' belongs to the physical vocabulary; then so also must the predicate 'x did not take place at Noosa Heads' belong to the physical vocabulary. But the predicate 'x did or did not take place at Noosa Heads' is true of every event, whether mental or physical.[5] We might rule out predicates that are tautologically true of every event, but this will not help since every event is truly describable either by 'x took place at Noosa Heads' or by 'x did not take place at Noosa Heads.' A different approach is needed.[6]

We may call those verbs mental that express propositional attitudes like believing, intending, desiring, hoping, knowing, perceiving, noticing, remembering, and so on. Such verbs are characterized by the fact that they sometimes feature in sentences with subjects that refer to persons, and are completed by embedded sentences in which the usual rules of substitution appear to break down. This criterion is not precise, since I do not want to include these verbs when they occur in contexts that are fully extensional ('He knows Paris,' 'He perceives the moon' may be cases), nor exclude them whenever they are not followed by embedded sentences. An alternative characterization of the desired class of mental verbs might be that they are psychological verbs as used when they create apparently nonextensional contexts.

Let us call a description of the form 'the event that is M' or an open sentence of the form 'event x is M' a *mental description* or a *mental open sentence* if and only if the expression that replaces 'M' contains at least one mental verb essentially. (Essentially, so as to rule out cases where the description or open sentence is logically equivalent to one not containing mental vocabulary.)

5. The point depends on assuming that mental events may intelligibly be said to have a location; but it is an assumption that must be true if an identity theory is, and here I am not trying to prove the theory but to formulate it.

6. I am indebted to Lee Bowie for emphasizing this difficulty.

Now we may say that an event is mental if and only if it has a mental description, or (the description operator not being primitive) if there is a mental open sentence true of that event alone. Physical events are those picked out by descriptions or open sentences that contain only the physical vocabulary essentially. It is less important to characterize a physical vocabulary because relative to the mental it is, so to speak, recessive in determining whether a description is mental or physical. (There will be some comments presently on the nature of a physical vocabulary, but these comments will fall far short of providing a criterion.)

On the proposed test of the mental, the distinguishing feature of the mental is not that it is private, subjective, or immaterial, but that it exhibits what Brentano called intentionality. Thus intentional actions are clearly included in the realm of the mental along with thoughts, hopes, and regrets (or the events tied to these). What may seem doubtful is whether the criterion will include events that have often been considered paradigmatic of the mental. Is it obvious, for example, that feeling a pain or seeing an afterimage will count as mental? Sentences that report such events seem free from taint of nonextensionality, and the same should be true of reports of raw feels, sense data, and other uninterpreted sensations, if there are any.

However, the criterion actually covers not only the havings of pains and afterimages, but much more besides. Take some event one would intuitively accept as physical, let's say the collision of two stars in distant space. There must be a purely physical predicate 'Px' true of this collision, and of others, but true of only this one at the time it occurred. This particular time, though, may be pinpointed as the same time that Jones notices that a pencil starts to roll across his desk. The distant stellar collision is thus *the* event x such that Px and x is simultaneous with Jones' noticing that a pencil starts to roll across his desk. The collision has now been picked out by a mental description and must be counted as a mental event.

This strategy will probably work to show every event to be

mental; we have obviously failed to capture the intuitive concept of the mental. It would be instructive to try to mend this trouble, but it is not necessary for present purposes. We can afford Spinozistic extravagance with the mental since accidental inclusions can only strengthen the hypothesis that all mental events are identical with physical events. What would matter would be failure to include bona fide mental events, but of this there seems to be no danger.

I want to describe, and presently to argue for, a version of the identity theory that denies that there can be strict laws connecting the mental and the physical. The very possibility of such a theory is easily obscured by the way in which identity theories are commonly defended and attacked. Charles Taylor, for example, agrees with protagonists of identity theories that the sole "ground" for accepting such theories is the supposition that correlations or laws can be established linking events described as mental with events described as physical. He says, "It is easy to see why this is so: unless a given mental event is invariably accompanied by a given, say, brain process, there is no ground for even mooting a general identity between the two."[7] Taylor goes on (correctly, I think) to allow that there may be identity without correlating laws, but my present interest is in noticing the invitation to confusion in the statement just quoted. What can "a given mental event" mean here? Not a particular, dated, event, for it would not make sense to speak of an individual event being "invariably accompanied" by another. Taylor is evidently thinking of events of a given *kind*. But if the only identities are of kinds of events, the identity theory presupposes correlating laws.

One finds the same tendency to build laws into the statement of the identity theory in these typical remarks:

When I say that a sensation is a brain process or that

7. Charles Taylor, "Mind-Body Identity, a Side Issue?" *The Philosophical Review*, LXXVI (1967), p. 202.

> lightning is an electrical discharge, I am using 'is' in the
> sense of strict identity . . . there are not two things: a flash
> of lightning and an electrical discharge. There is one thing,
> a flash of lightning, which is described scientifically as an
> electrical discharge to the earth from a cloud of ionized
> water molecules.[8]

The last sentence of this quotation is perhaps to be understood as
saying that for every lightning flash there exists an electrical dis-
charge to the earth from a cloud of ionized water molecules with
which it is identical. Here we have a honest ontology of individual events and can make literal sense of identity. We can
also see how there could be identities without correlating laws.
It is possible, however, to have an ontology of events with the
conditions of individuation specified in such a way that any
identity implies a correlating law. Kim, for example, suggests that
Fa and Gb "describe or refer to the same event" if and only if
$a = b$ and the property of being F = the property of being G.
The identity of the properties in turn entails that (x) $(Fx \leftrightarrow Gx)$.[9]
No wonder Kim says:

> If pain is identical with brain state B, there must be a con-
> comitance between occurrences of pain and occurrences of
> brain state B. . . . Thus, a necessary condition of the pain-
> brain state B identity is that the two expressions 'being in
> pain' and 'being in brain state B' have the same extension.

8. J. J. C. Smart, "Sensations and Brain Processes," *The Philosophical Review*, LXVIII (1959), pp. 141–56. The quoted passages are on pp. 163–165
of the reprinted version in *The Philosophy of Mind*, ed. V. C. Chappell
(Englewood Cliffs, N. J., 1962). For another example, see David K. Lewis,
"An Argument for the Identity Theory," *The Journal of Philosophy*, LXIII
(1966), pp. 17–25. Here the assumption is made explicit when Lewis takes
events as universals (p. 17, footnotes 1 and 2). I do not suggest that Smart
and Lewis are confused, only that their way of stating the identity theory
tends to obscure the distinction between particular events and kinds of
events on which the formulation of my theory depends.

9. Jaegwon Kim, "On the Psycho-Physical Identity Theory," *American
Philosophical Quarterly*, III (1966), p. 231.

... There is no conceivable observation that would confirm or refute the identity but not the associated correlation.[10]

It may make the situation clearer to give a fourfold classification of theories of the relation between mental and physical events that emphasizes the independence of claims about laws and claims of identity. On the one hand there are those who assert, and those who deny, the existence of psychophysical laws; on the other hand there are those who say mental events are identical with physical and those who deny this. Theories are thus divided into four sorts: *Nomological monism*, which affirms that there are correlating laws and that the events correlated are one (materialists belong in this category); *nomological dualism*, which comprises various forms of parallelism, interactionism, and epiphenomenalism; *anomalous dualism*, which combines ontological dualism with the general failure of laws correlating the mental and the physical (Cartesianism). And finally there is *anomalous monism*, which classifies the position I wish to occupy.[11]

Anomalous monism resembles materialism in its claim that all events are physical, but rejects the thesis, usually considered essential to materialism, that mental phenomena can be given

10. Ibid., pp. 227-28. Richard Brandt and Jaegwon Kim propose roughly the same criterion in "The Logic of the Identity Theory," *The Journal of Philosophy* LIV (1967), pp. 515-537. They remark that on their conception of event identity, the identity theory "makes a stronger claim than merely that there is a pervasive phenomenal-physical correlation" (p. 518). I do not discuss the stronger claim.

11. Anomalous monism is more or less explicitly recognized as a possible position by Herbert Feigl, "The 'Mental' and the 'Physical,'" in *Concepts, Theories and the Mind-Body Problem*, vol. II, *Minnesota Studies in the Philosophy of Science* (Minneapolis, 1958); Sydney Shoemaker, "Ziff's Other Minds," *The Journal of Philosophy*, LXII (1965), p. 589; David Randall Luce, "Mind-Body Identity and Psycho-Physical Correlation," *Philosophical Studies*, XVII (1966), pp. 1-7; Charles Taylor, op. cit., p. 207. Something like my position is tentatively accepted by Thomas Nagel, "Physicalism," *The Philosophical Review*, LXXIV (1965), pp. 339-356, and briefly endorsed by P. F. Strawson in *Freedom and the Will*, ed. D. F. Pears (London, 1963), pp. 63-67.

purely physical explanations. Anomalous monism shows an ontological bias only in that it allows the possibility that not all events are mental, while insisting that all events are physical. Such a bland monism, unbuttressed by correlating laws or conceptual economies, does not seem to merit the term "reductionism"; in any case it is not apt to inspire the nothing-but reflex ("Conceiving the *Art of the Fugue* was nothing but a complex neural event," and so forth).

Although the position I describe denies there are psychophysical laws, it is consistent with the view that mental characteristics are in some sense dependent, or supervenient, on physical characteristics. Such supervenience might be taken to mean that there cannot be two events alike in all physical respects but differing in some mental respect, or that an object cannot alter in some mental respect without altering in some physical respect. Dependence or supervenience of this kind does not entail reducibility through law or definition: if it did, we could reduce moral properties to descriptive, and this there is good reason to *believe* cannot be done; and we might be able to reduce truth in a formal system to syntactical properties, and this we *know* cannot in general be done.

This last example is in useful analogy with the sort of lawless monism under consideration. Think of the physical vocabulary as the entire vocabulary of some language L with resources adequate to express a certain amount of mathematics, and its own syntax. L' is L augmented with the truth predicate 'true-in-L,' which is "mental." In L (and hence L') it is possible to pick out, with a definite description or open sentence, each sentence in the extension of the truth predicate, but if L is consistent there exists no predicate of syntax (of the "physical" vocabulary), no matter how complex, that applies to all and only the true sentences of L. There can be no "psychophysical law" in the form of a biconditional, '(x) (x is true-in-L if and only if x is ϕ)' where 'ϕ' is replaced by a "physical" predicate (a predicate of L). Similarly, we can pick out each mental event using the physical vocabulary alone, but no purely physical predicate, no matter how complex, has, as a matter of law, the same extension as a mental predicate.

It should now be evident how anomalous monism reconciles the three original principles. Causality and identity are relations between individual events no matter how described. But laws are linguistic; and so events can instantiate laws, and hence be explained or predicted in the light of laws, only as those events are described in one or another way. The principle of causal interaction deals with events in extension and is therefore blind to the mental-physical dichotomy. The principle of the anomalism of the mental concerns events described as mental, for events are mental only as described. The principle of the nomological character of causality must be read carefully: it says that when events are related as cause and effect, they have descriptions that instantiate a law. It does not say that every true singular statement of causality instantiates a law.[12]

II

The analogy just bruited, between the place of the mental amid the physical, and the place of the semantical in a world of syntax, should not be strained. Tarski proved that a consistent language cannot (under some natural assumptions) contain an open sentence 'Fx' true of all and only the true sentences of that language. If our analogy were pressed, then we would expect a proof that there can be no physical open sentence 'Px' true of all and only the events having some mental property. In fact, however, nothing I can say about the irreducibility of the mental deserves to be called a proof; and the kind of irreducibility is

12. The point that substitutivity of identity fails in the context of explanation is made in connection with the present subject by Norman Malcolm, "Scientific Materialism and the Identity Theory," *Dialogue*, III (1964–65), pp. 123–124. See also my "Actions, Reasons and Causes," *The Journal of Philosophy*, LX (1963), pp. 696–699 and "The Individuation of Events" in *Essays in Honor of Carl G. Hempel*, ed. N. Rescher, et al. (Dordrecht, 1969).

different. For if anomalous monism is correct, not only can every mental event be uniquely singled out using only physical concepts, but since the number of events that falls under each mental predicate may, for all we know, be finite, there may well exist a physical open sentence coextensive with each mental predicate, though to construct it might involve the tedium of a lengthy and uninstructive alternation. Indeed, even if finitude is not assumed, there seems no compelling reason to deny that there could be coextensive predicates, one mental and one physical.

The thesis is rather that the mental is nomologically irreducible: there may be *true* general statements relating the mental and the physical, statements that have the logical form of a law; but they are not *lawlike* (in a strong sense to be described). If by absurdly remote chance we were to stumble on a nonstochastic true psychophysical generalization, we would have no reason to believe it more than roughly true.

Do we, by declaring that there are no (strict) psychophysical laws, poach on the empirical preserves of science—a form of *hubris* against which philosophers are often warned? Of course, to judge a statement lawlike or illegal is not to decide its truth outright; relative to the acceptance of a general statement on the basis of instances, ruling it lawlike must be a priori. But such relative apriorism does not in itself justify philosophy, for in general the grounds for deciding to trust a statement on the basis of its instances will in turn be governed by theoretical and empirical concerns not to be distinguished from those of science. If the case of supposed laws linking the mental and the physical is different, it can only be because to allow the possibility of such laws would amount to changing the subject. By changing the subject I mean here: deciding not to accept the criterion of the mental in terms of the vocabulary of the propositional attitudes. This short answer cannot prevent further ramifications of the problem, however, for there is no clear line between changing the subject and changing what one says on an old subject, which is to admit, in the present context at least, that there is no clear line between philosophy and science. Where there are no fixed boundaries only the timid never risk trespass.

It will sharpen our appreciation of the anomological character of mental-physical generalizations to consider a related matter, the failure of definitional behaviorism. Why are we willing (as I assume we are) to abandon the attempt to give explicit definitions of mental concepts in terms of behavioral ones? Not, surely, just because all actual tries are conspicuously inadequate. Rather it is because we are persuaded, as we are in the case of so many other forms of definitional reductionism (naturalism in ethics, instrumentalism and operationalism in the sciences, the causal theory of meaning, phenomenalism, and so on—the catalogue of philosophy's defeats), that there is system in the failures. Suppose we try to say, not using any mental concepts, what it is for a man to believe there is life on Mars. One line we could take is this: when a certain sound is produced in the man's presence ("Is there life on Mars?") he produces another ("Yes"). But of course this shows he believes there is life on Mars only if he understands English, his production of the sound was intentional, and was a response to the sounds as meaning something in English; and so on. For each discovered deficiency, we add a new proviso. Yet no matter how we patch and fit the nonmental conditions, we always find the need for an additional condition (provided he *notices, understands,* etc.) that is mental in character.[13]

A striking feature of attempts at definitional reduction is how little seems to hinge on the question of synonymy between definiens and definiendum. Of course, by imagining counterexamples we do discredit claims of synonymy. But the pattern of failure prompts a stronger conclusion: if we were to find an open sentence couched in behavioral terms and exactly coextensive with some mental predicate, nothing could reasonably persuade us that we had found it. We know too much about thought and be-

---

13. The theme is developed in Roderick Chisholm, *Perceiving* (Ithaca, New York, 1957), chap. 11.

havior to trust exact and universal statements linking them. Beliefs and desires issue in behavior only as modified and mediated by further beliefs and desires, attitudes and attendings, without limit. Clearly this holism of the mental realm is a clue both to the autonomy and to the anomalous character of the mental.

These remarks apropos definitional behaviorism provide at best hints of why we should not expect nomological connections between the mental and the physical. The central case invites further consideration.

Lawlike statements are general statements that support counterfactual and subjunctive claims, and are supported by their instances. There is (in my view) no nonquestion-begging criterion of the lawlike, which is not to say there are no reasons in particular cases for a judgment. Lawlikeness is a matter of degree, which is not to deny that there may be cases beyond debate. And within limits set by the conditions of communication, there is room for much variation between individuals in the pattern of statements to which various degrees of nomologicality are assigned. In all these respects, nomologicality is much like analyticity, as one might expect since both are linked to meaning.

'All emeralds are green' is lawlike in that its instances confirm it, but 'all emeralds are grue' is not, for 'grue' means 'observed before time t and green, otherwise blue,' and if our observations were all made before t and uniformly revealed green emeralds, this would not be a reason to expect other emeralds to be blue. Nelson Goodman has suggested that this shows that some predicates, 'grue' for example, are unsuited to laws (and thus a criterion of suitable predicates could lead to a criterion of the lawlike). But it seems to me the anomalous character of 'All emeralds are grue' shows only that the predicates 'is an emerald' and 'is grue' are not suited to one another: grueness is not an inductive property of emeralds. Grueness *is* however an inductive property of entities of other sorts, for instance of emerires. (Something is an emerire if it is examined before t and is an emerald, and otherwise is a sapphire.) Not only is 'All emerires are grue' entailed by the conjunction of the lawlike statements 'All emeralds are green' and 'All sapphires are blue,' but there is no reason, as far as I can see, to reject the deliverance of intuition, that it is itself lawlike.[14] Nomological statements bring together predicates that we know a priori are made for each other—know, that is, independently of knowing whether the evidence supports a connection between them. 'Blue,' 'red,' and 'green' are made for emeralds, sapphires, and roses; 'grue,' 'bleen,' and 'gred' are made for sapphalds, emerires, and emeroses.

The direction in which the discussion seems headed is this: mental and physical predicates are not made for one another. In point of lawlikeness, psychophysical statements are more like 'All emeralds are grue' than like 'All emeralds are green.'

Before this claim is plausible, it must be seriously modified. The fact that emeralds examined before *t* are grue not only is no reason to believe all emeralds are grue; it is not even a reason (if we know the time) to believe *any* unobserved emeralds are grue. But if an event of a certain mental sort has usually been accompanied by an event of a certain physical sort, this often is a good reason to expect other cases to follow suit roughly in proportion. The generalizations that embody such practical wisdom are assumed to be only roughly true, or they are explicitly stated in probabilistic terms, or they are insulated from counter-example by generous escape clauses. Their importance lies mainly in the support they lend singular causal claims and related explanations of particular events. The support derives from the fact that such a generalization, however crude and vague, may provide good reason to believe that underlying the particular case there

14. This view is accepted by Richard C. Jeffrey, "Goodman's Query," *The Journal of Philosophy,* LXII (1966), p. 286 ff., John R. Wallace, "Goodman, Logic, Induction," same journal and issue, p. 318, and John M. Vickers, "Characteristics of Projectible Predicates," *The Journal of Philosophy,* LXIV (1967), p. 285. On pp. 328–329 and 286–287 of these journal issues respectively Goodman disputes the lawlikeness of statements like "All emerires are grue." I cannot see, however, that he meets the point of my "Emeroses by Other Names," *The Journal of Philosophy,* LXIII (1966), pp. 778–780.

is a regularity that could be formulated sharply and without caveat.

In our daily traffic with events and actions that must be foreseen or understood, we perforce make use of the sketchy summary generalization, for we do not know a more accurate law, or if we do, we lack a description of the particular events in which we are interested that would show the relevance of the law. But there is an important distinction to be made within the category of the rude rule of thumb. On the one hand, there are generalizations whose positive instances give us reason to believe the generalization itself could be improved by adding further provisos and conditions stated in the same general vocabulary as the original generalization. Such a generalization points to the form and vocabulary of the finished law: we may say that it is a *homonomic* generalization. On the other hand there are generalizations which when instantiated may give us reason to believe there is a precise law at work, but one that can be stated only by shifting to a different vocabulary. We may call such generalizations *heteronomic*.

I suppose most of our practical lore (and science) is heteronomic. This is because a law can hope to be precise, explicit, and as exceptionless as possible only if it draws its concepts from a comprehensive closed theory. This ideal theory may or may not be deterministic, but it is if any true theory is. Within the physical sciences we do find homonomic generalizations, generalizations such that if the evidence supports them, we then have reason to believe they may be sharpened indefinitely by drawing upon further physical concepts: there is a theoretical asymptote of perfect coherence with all the evidence, perfect predictability (under the terms of the system), total explanation (again under the terms of the system). Or perhaps the ultimate theory is probabilistic, and the asymptote is less than perfection; but in that case there will be no better to be had.

Confidence that a statement is homonomic, correctible within its own conceptual domain, demands that it draw its concepts from a theory with strong constitutive elements. Here is the simplest possible illustration; if the lesson carries, it will be obvious that the simplification could be mended.

The measurement of length, weight, temperature, or time depends (among many other things, of course) on the existence in each case of a two-place relation that is transitive and asymmetric: warmer than, later than, heavier than, and so forth. Let us take the relation *longer than* as our example. The law or postulate of transitivity is this:

$$(\text{L}) \qquad \text{L}(x,y) \text{ and } \text{L}(y,z) \rightarrow \text{L}(x,z)$$

Unless this law (or some sophisticated variant) holds, we cannot easily make sense of the concept of length. There will be no way of assigning numbers to register even so much as ranking in length, let alone the more powerful demands of measurement on a ratio scale. And this remark goes not only for any three items directly involved in an intransitivity: it is easy to show (given a few more assumptions essential to measurement of length) that there is no consistent assignment of a ranking to any item unless (L) holds in full generality.

Clearly (L) alone cannot exhaust the import of 'longer than'—otherwise it would not differ from 'warmer than' or 'later than.' We must suppose there is some empirical content, however difficult to formulate in the available vocabulary, that distinguishes 'longer than' from the other two-place transitive predicates of measurement and on the basis of which we may assert that one thing is longer than another. Imagine this empirical content to be partly given by the predicate '$\text{o}(x,y)$'. So we have this "meaning postulate":

$$(\text{M}) \qquad \text{o}(x,y) \rightarrow \text{L}(x,y)$$

that partly interprets (L). But now (L) and (M) together yield an empirical theory of great strength, for together they entail that there do not exist three objects a, b, and c such that $\text{o}(a,b)$, $\text{o}(b,c)$, and $\text{o}(c,a)$. Yet what is to prevent this happening if '$\text{o}(x,y)$ is a predicate we can ever, with confidence, apply? Suppose we *think* we observe an intransitive triad; what do we say? We could count (L) false, but then we would have no application for the concept of length. We could say (M) gives a wrong test for length; but then it is unclear what we thought was the *content* of the idea of one thing being longer than another. Or we could say that the objects under observation are not, as the theory requires, *rigid* objects. It is a mistake to think we are forced to accept some one of these answers. Concepts such as that of length are sustained in equilibrium by a number of conceptual pressures, and theories of fundamental measurement are distorted if we force the decision, among such principles as (L) and (M): analytic or synthetic. It is better to say the whole set of axioms, laws, or postulates for the measurement of length is partly constitutive of the idea of a system of macroscopic, rigid, physical objects. I suggest that the existence of lawlike statements in physical science depends upon the existence of constitutive (or synthetic a priori) laws like those of the measurement of length within the same conceptual domain.

Just as we cannot intelligibly assign a length to any object unless a comprehensive theory holds of objects of that sort, we cannot intelligibly attribute any propositional attitude to an agent except within the framework of a viable theory of his beliefs, desires, intentions, and decisions.

There is no assigning beliefs to a person one by one on the basis of his verbal behavior, his choices, or other local signs no matter how plain and evident, for we make sense of particular beliefs only as they cohere with other beliefs, with preferences, with intentions, hopes, fears, expectations, and the rest. It is not merely, as with the measurement of length, that each case tests a theory and depends upon it, but that the content of a propositional attitude derives from its place in the pattern.

Crediting people with a large degree of consistency cannot be counted mere charity: it is unavoidable if we are to be in a position to accuse them meaningfully of error and some degree of irrationality. Global confusion, like universal mistake, is unthinkable, not because imagination boggles, but because too much confusion leaves nothing to be confused about and massive error erodes the background of true belief against which alone failure can be construed. To appreciate the limits to the kind and amount of blunder and bad thinking we can intelligibly pin on others is to see once more the inseparability of the question what concepts a person commands and the question what he does with those concepts in the way of belief, desire, and intention. To the extent that we fail to discover a coherent and plausible pattern in the attitudes and actions of others we simply forego the chance of treating them as persons.

The problem is not bypassed but given center stage by appeal to explicit speech behavior. For we could not begin to decode a man's sayings if we could not make out his attitudes towards his sentences, such as holding, wishing, or wanting them to be true. Beginning from these attitudes, we must work out a theory of what he means, thus simultaneously giving content to his attitudes and to his words. In our need to make him make sense, we will try for a theory that finds him consistent, a believer of truths, and a lover of the good (all by our own lights, it goes without saying). Life being what it is, there will be no simple theory that fully meets these demands. Many theories will effect a more or less acceptable compromise, and between these theories there may be no objective grounds for choice.

The heteronomic character of general statements linking the mental and the physical traces back to this central role of translation in the description of all propositional attitudes, and to the indeterminacy of translation.[15] There are no strict psychophysical laws because of the disparate commitments of the mental and physical schemes. It is a feature of physical reality that physical change can be explained by laws that connect it with other changes and conditions physically described. It is a feature of the mental that the attribution of mental phenomena must be

15. The influence of W. V. Quine's doctrine of the indeterminacy of translation, as in chap. 2 of *Word and Object* (Cambridge, Mass., 1960), is, I hope, obvious. In § 45 Quine develops the connection between translation and the propositional attitudes, and remarks that "Brentano's thesis of the irreducibility of intentional idioms is of a piece with the thesis of indeterminacy of translation" (p. 221).

responsible to the background of reasons, beliefs, and intentions of the individual. There cannot be tight connections between the realms if each is to retain allegiance to its proper source of evidence. The nomological irreducibility of the mental does not derive merely from the seamless nature of the world of thought, preference and intention, for such interdependence is common to physical theory, and is compatible with there being a single right way of interpreting a man's attitudes without relativization to a scheme of translation. Nor is the irreducibility due simply to the possibility of many equally eligible schemes, for this is compatible with an arbitrary choice of one scheme relative to which assignments of mental traits are made. The point is rather that when we use the concepts of belief, desire and the rest, we must stand prepared, as the evidence accumulates, to adjust our theory in the light of considerations of overall cogency: the constitutive ideal of rationality partly controls each phase in the evolution of what must be an evolving theory. An arbitrary choice of translation scheme would preclude such opportunistic tempering of theory; put differently, a right arbitrary choice of a translation manual would be of a manual acceptable in the light of all possible evidence, and this is a choice we cannot make. We must conclude, I think, that nomological slack between the mental and the physical is essential as long as we conceive of man as a rational animal.

III

The gist of the foregoing discussion, as well as its conclusion, will be familiar. That there is a categorial difference between the mental and the physical is a commonplace. It may seem odd that I say nothing of the supposed privacy of the mental, or the special authority an agent has with respect to his own propositional attitudes, but this appearance of novelty would fade if we were to investigate in more detail the grounds for accepting a scheme of translation. The step from the categorial difference between the mental and the physical to the impossibility of strict laws relating them is less common, but certainly not new. If there is a surprise, then, it will be to find the lawlessness of the mental serving to help establish the identity of the mental with that paradigm of the lawlike, the physical.

The reasoning is this. We are assuming, under the Principle of the Causal Dependence of the Mental, that some mental events at least are causes or effects of physical events; the argument applies only to these. A second Principle (of the Nomological Character of Causality) says that each true singular causal statement is backed by a strict law connecting events of kinds to which the events mentioned as cause and effect belong. Where there are rough, but homonomic, laws, there are laws drawing on concepts from the same conceptual domain and upon which there is no improving in point of precision and comprehensiveness. We urged in the last section that such laws occur in the physical sciences. Physical theory promises to provide a comprehensive closed system guaranteed to yield a standardized, unique description of every physical event couched in a vocabulary amenable to law.

It is not plausible that mental concepts alone can provide such a framework, simply because the mental does not, by our first principle, constitute a closed system. Too much happens to affect the mental that is not itself a systematic part of the mental. But if we combine this observation with the conclusion that no psychophysical statement is, or can be built into, a strict law, we have the Principle of the Anomalism of the Mental: there are no strict laws at all on the basis of which we can predict and explain mental phenomena.

The demonstration of identity follows easily. Suppose m, a mental event, caused p, a physical event; then under some description m and p instantiate a strict law. This law can only be physical, according to the previous paragraph. But if m falls under a physical law, it has a physical description; which is to say it is a physical event. An analogous argument works when a physical event causes a mental event. So every mental event that is causally related to a physical event is a physical event. In order to establish anomalous monism in full generality it would be sufficient to show that every mental event is cause or effect of some physical event; I shall not attempt this.

If one event causes another, there is a strict law which those events instantiate when properly described. But it is possible (and typical) to know of the singular causal relation without knowing the law or the relevant descriptions. Knowledge requires reasons, but these are available in the form of rough heteronomic generalizations, which are lawlike in that instances make it reasonable to expect other instances to follow suit without being lawlike in the sense of being indefinitely refinable. Applying these facts to knowledge of identities, we see that it is possible to know that a mental event is identical with some physical event without knowing which one (in the sense of being able to give it a unique physical description that brings it under a relevant law). Even if someone knew the entire physical history of the world, and every mental event were identical with a physical, it would not follow that he could predict or explain a single mental event (so described, of course).

Two features of mental events in their relation to the physical—causal dependence and nomological independence—combine, then, to dissolve what has often seemed a paradox, the efficacy of thought and purpose in the material world, and their freedom from law. When we portray events as perceivings, rememberings, decisions and actions, we necessarily locate them amid physical happenings through the relation of cause and effect; but that same mode of portrayal insulates mental events, as long as we do not change the idiom, from the strict laws that can in principle be called upon to explain and predict physical phenomena.

Mental events as a class cannot be explained by physical science; particular mental events can when we know particular identities. But the explanations of mental events in which we are typically interested relate them to other mental events and conditions. We explain a man's free actions, for example, by appeal to his desires, habits, knowledge and perceptions. Such accounts of intentional behavior operate in a conceptual framework removed from the direct reach of physical law by describing both cause and effect, reason and action, as aspects of a portrait of a human agent. The anomalism of the mental is thus a necessary condition for viewing action as autonomous. I conclude with a second passage from Kant:

> It is an indispensable problem of speculative philosophy to show that its illusion respecting the contradiction rests on this, that we think of man in a different sense and relation when we call him free, and when we regard him as subject to the laws of nature. . . . It must therefore show that not only can both of these very well co-exist, but that both must be thought *as necessarily united* in the same subject. . . .[16]

16. Op. cit., p. 76.

Roderick M. Chisholm
On the Nature of Empirical Evidence

THE PRESENT paper[1] is divided into four parts. The first is a sketch of what I take to be the basic concepts and principles of epistemic logic; the second is concerned with evidential support; the third is concerned with the problem of defining knowledge; and the fourth is an attempt to formulate criteria of application for some of the concepts of the theory of evidence. Much of what I have to say is by way of correction and emendation of what was said in my book *Theory of Knowledge* (Englewood Cliffs, N. J., 1966). I choose this occasion to make these corrections and emendations, since the topic is basic to the question of "Experience and Theory" and since I wish to deal with problems that have been pointed out by Professor Gettier and Professor Heidelberger of the University of Massachusetts.[2]

I

We may think of the theory of evidence as a branch of the theory of preference, or, more accurately, of the theory of *right* preference, or preferability. Let us take *epistemic preferability* as our undefined epistemic concept. Thus we begin with the locution, "*p* is epistemically preferable to *q* for S at *t*," where the expressions occupying the place of "*p*" and "*q*" are terms referring to states of affairs (or propositions) and where "*S*" and "*t*," respectively, refer to a particular person and to a particular time. The following six principles are axioms of epistemic preferability.

1. I am indebted to Herbert Heidelberger, Ernest Sosa, Robert Swartz, Edmund Gettier, and Robert Keim for criticisms of earlier versions of this paper.

2. See Edmund L. Gettier, "Is Justified True Belief Knowledge?" *Analysis*, XXIII (1963), pp. 121–123, and Herbert Heidelberger, "Chisholm's Epistemic Principles," *Nous*, III (1969), pp. 73–82.

1) Epistemic preferability, like other types of preferability, is such that, for any states of affairs *p* and *q*, if *p* is preferable to *q* for *S* at *t*, then it is not the case that *q* is preferable to *p* for *S* at *t*. (2) Again like other types of preferability, epistemic preferability is such that, for any states of affairs, *p*, *q*, and *r*, if it is not the case that *p* is preferable to *q*, and if it is not the case that *q* is preferable to *r*, then it is not the case that *p* is preferable to *r*. (3) For any propositions *h* and *i*, believing *h* is epistemically preferable to believing *i* for *S* at *t*, if and only if, believing *not-i* is epistemically preferable to believing *not-h* for *S* at *t*.[3] (4) For any proposition *h*, if withholding *h* (that is, neither believing *h* nor believing *not-h*) is *not* epistemically preferable to believing *h*, then believing *h* is epistemically preferable to believing *not-h*. "If agnosticism is not epistemically preferable to theism, then theism is epistemically preferable to atheism." (5) For any propositions *h* and *i*, withholding *h* is the same in epistemic value as withholding *i* for *S* at *t*, if and only if, either believing *h* is the same in epistemic value as believing *i* for *S* at *t* or believing *not-h* is the same in epistemic value as believing *i* for *S* at *t*. (To say that one state of affairs is "the same in epistemic value" as another is to say that neither one is epistemically preferable to the other.) And (6) for any propositions *h* and *i*, if believing *i* is epistemically preferable to believing *h* for *S* at *t* and also epistemically preferable to believing *not-h* for *S* at *t*, then withholding *h* is

---

3. I have called the terms of the relation of epistemic preferability "propositions or states of affairs" and I have used the letters as *"p," "q,"* and *"r"* as variables designating such terms. I have called the objects of such attitudes as believing "propositions" and have used the letters as *"h," "i,"* and *"j"* to designate such objects. I believe, however, that the entities which are called in the one case "propositions or states of affairs" and in the other "propositions" are one and the same, but this belief is not essential to any of the points of the present paper. Some further defense of it may be found in my paper, "Language, Logic, and States of Affairs," in Sidney Hook ed., *Language and Philosophy* (New York, 1969), pp. 241–248, and in "Events and Propositions," *Nous*, iv (1970).

epistemically preferable to withholding i for S at t.[4]

In order to explicate the basic concepts of the theory of epistemic preferability, let us consider what is involved in asking, for any given proposition and any given subject and any given time, which is epistemically preferable: believing the proposition, disbelieving the proposition (that is, believing the negation of the proposition), or withholding the proposition (neither believing nor disbelieving the proposition). We may consider six different states of affairs which, together with their negations, give us twelve possibilities.

a) The proposition may be such that believing it is epistemically preferable to withholding it (for the particular subject at the particular time). In this case, we may say that the proposition (for that subject at that time) is one that is *beyond reasonable doubt*, or, as we may put it more briefly, one that is *reasonable*. The propositions falling within the negation of this category are those which are such that believing them is *not* epistemically preferable to withholding them. Let us say that such propositions are epistemically *gratuitous*.[5]

b) The proposition may be such that believing it is epistemically preferable to disbelieving it (believing its negation). Let us say that a proposition of this sort is one that has *some presumption in*

4. These axioms are used in a forthcoming work on epistemic logic by Roderick M. Chisholm, Ernest Sosa, and Robert Keim. The fifth and sixth were proposed by Mr. Keim. Versions of the others may be found in: *Theory of Knowledge*, p. 22n; Roderick M. Chisholm, "The Principles of Epistemic Appraisal," in *Current Philosophical Issues: Essays in Honor of Curt John Ducasse*, ed. F. C. Dommeyer (Springfield, Illinois, 1966), pp. 87–104, and "On a Principle of Epistemic Preferability," *Philosophy and Phenomenological Research*, xxx (1969); and Roderick M. Chisholm and Ernest Sosa, "On the Logic of 'Intrinsically Better,'" *American Philosophical Quarterly*, iii (1966), pp. 244–249.

5. If we use "reasonable" as short for "beyond reasonable doubt," we should avoid using "unreasonable" as short for "not beyond reasonable doubt." For "unreasonable" suggests "unacceptable," to be defined below, rather than "gratuitous."

its favor. The phrase "more probable than not" is sometimes used to express this concept. Our principles imply that whatever is thus beyond reasonable doubt also has some presumption in its favor, but they do not imply the converse. Propositions falling within the negation of this second category—propositions which are such that believing them is not epistemically preferable to disbelieving them—will be such as to have no presumption in their favor.

c) The proposition may be such that withholding it is epistemically preferable to believing it. Let us say that a proposition of this sort is one that is *unacceptable.* Hence any proposition not such that withholding it is epistemically preferable to believing may be said to be *acceptable.* Our principles imply that any acceptable proposition is a proposition that has some presumption in its favor, but they do not imply the converse. They also imply that any proposition that is beyond reasonable doubt is one that is acceptable, but again they do not imply the converse. Hence we have the beginnings of an epistemic hierarchy. (The hierarchy may be illustrated as follows. If the police are justified in detaining you, then the proposition that you did the deed should be one which, for them, has some presumption in its favor. If the state is justified in bringing you to trial, then that proposition should be one which, for it, is acceptable. And if the jury is justified in finding you guilty, then the proposition should be one which, for it, is beyond reasonable doubt.)

d) The proposition may be such that withholding it is epistemically preferable to disbelieving it. Hence any proposition falling within this category is one having an unacceptable negation. And any proposition falling within the negation of this category—any proposition such that withholding it is not epistemically preferable to disbelieving it—is one that has an acceptable negation.

e) The proposition may be such that disbelieving it is epistemically preferable to believing it. In this case, the negation of the proposition is such that there is some presumption in its favor. And any proposition falling within the negation of this category will be one such that there is no presumption in favor of its negation.

f) Finally, the proposition may be such that disbelieving it is epistemically preferable to withholding it. In this case, the negation of the proposition will be beyond reasonable doubt and the proposition itself, therefore, will be unacceptable. A proposition falling within the negation of this category will be one that has a gratuitous negation.

If we use "Bh" for "believing h," "$B{\sim}h$" for "believing *not-h*" (or "disbelieving h"), "Wh" for "withholding h," and "——P . . ." for "——is epistemically preferable to . . . for S at t," then the following formulae will illustrate the categories just discussed:

a) $(Bh)P(Wh)$ d) $(Wh)P(B{\sim}h)$
b) $(Bh)P(B{\sim}h)$ e) $(B{\sim}h)P(Bh)$
c) $(Wh)P(Bh)$ f) $(B{\sim}h)P(Wh)$.

We may use the letters, "a," "b," "c," "d," "e," and "f," respectively, as further abbreviations for these six formulae, and "${\sim}a$," "${\sim}b$," "${\sim}c$," "${\sim}d$," "${\sim}e$," and "${\sim}f$," respectively, as abbreviations for their negations.

Some of the consequences of our first and fourth axioms may now be abbreviated as follows:

a implies: $b,\ {\sim}c,\ d,\ {\sim}e,\ f$

b implies: $d,\ {\sim}e,\ {\sim}f$

c implies: ${\sim}a$

d implies: ${\sim}f$

e implies: ${\sim}a,\ {\sim}b,\ c$

f implies: ${\sim}a,\ {\sim}b,\ c,\ {\sim}d,\ e$

${\sim}b$ implies: ${\sim}a,\ c$

${\sim}c$ implies: $b,\ d,\ {\sim}e,\ {\sim}f$

${\sim}d$ implies: ${\sim}a,\ {\sim}b,\ c,\ e$

${\sim}e$ implies: $d,\ {\sim}f$.

These formulae thus exhibit some of the relations holding among the various epistemic concepts defined above. For example, since ${\sim}c$ implies d (that is, since any proposition which is such that withholding it is not epistemically preferable to believing it is also one which is such that withholding it is preferable to disbelieving it), we may say that if a proposition is acceptable then it has an unacceptable negation. Hence any proposition is such that either it or its negation is unacceptable.

Making use of some of the terms just defined, we may introduce still other epistemic categories. Thus we may say that a proposition is *counterbalanced* if there is no presumption in its favor and also no presumption in favor of its negation. In other words, a proposition is counterbalanced, for S at t, if believing it is not epistemically preferable to disbelieving it for S at t and if disbelieving it is not epistemically preferable to believing it for S at t. In still other words, h is counterbalanced if believing h and believing *not-h* are the same in epistemic value. We may say that a proposition *ought to be withheld* provided that both it and its negation are unacceptable. Our principles imply the Pyrrhonistic thesis according to which any proposition that is counterbalanced is also one that ought to be withheld.

The term "indifferent" is sometimes taken in the present sense of the term "counterbalanced"; in the book, *Theory of Knowledge*, I defined it in this way. But "indifferent" is sometimes taken, in analogy with one of its uses in ethics and deontic logic, to suggest that, if a proposition is thus indifferent to a man, then the doxastic attitude (believing, disbelieving, or withholding) that he may take toward the proposition is one that "does not matter." If we are right in saying that every proposition is such that either it or its negation is unacceptable, then, although there are many propositions that might be said to be "indifferent" in the first sense, there are no propositions that may be said to be "indifferent" in the second. Hence we shall avoid the term in the present discussion.

We do not yet have a characterization of *the evident*. Any proposition that is evident, of course, is also one that is beyond reasonable doubt. But it is not the case that any proposition that is beyond reasonable doubt is also one that is evident. Thus an inductive argument may establish beyond reasonable doubt that the next ball to be drawn from a certain urn is one that is red, but it may not be evident that that ball is red until the drawing is made and the ball examined. Hence the evident is even higher in our epistemic hierarchy than that which is beyond reasonable doubt.

Among possible definitions of "h is evident for S at t," in terms of our undefined epistemic concept are these:

1) h is beyond reasonable doubt for S at t, and there is no proposition i such that believing i is epistemically preferable to believing h for S at t.

2) h is beyond reasonable doubt for S at t, and believing that he exists is not epistemically preferable to believing h for S at t.

3) h is beyond reasonable doubt for S at t, and there is no tautology or logical truth such that believing it is epistemically preferable to believing h for S at t.

4) h is beyond reasonable doubt for S at t, and there is no proposition i such that disbelieving the conjunction, i and not-i, is epistemically preferable to believing h for S at t.

Unless we are willing to restrict the concept of the evident, and therefore also the concept of knowledge, to a small group of subjective propositions and logical truths, we should reject these first four possibilities as being too rigid. (They could be used, however, to define various technical senses of the term "certain.") I suggest that we define "the evident" by reference to the following:

5) For every proposition i, believing h is epistemically preferable to withholding i for S at t.

Such a definition would imply that, if h is evident, then h is also beyond reasonable doubt, for it would imply that believing h is epistemically preferable to withholding h. (One could weaken the definition by saying instead, "withholding i is not epistemically preferable to believing h," but I believe that the definition, so weakened, would not capture the concept of the evident.)

We will now list the definitions we have proposed for the basic concepts of the theory of evidence.

D1) h is *beyond reasonable doubt* for S at t = Df Believing h is epistemically preferable to withholding h for S at t (that is, formula a is true).

D2) h is *gratuitous* for S at t = Df Believing h is not epistemically preferable to withholding h for S at t (that is, formula a is false).

D3) There is *some presumption in favor* of h for S at t = Df Believing h is epistemically preferable to believing *not-h* for S at t (that is, formula b is true).

D4) h is *unacceptable* for S at t = Df Withholding h is epistemically preferable to believing h for S at t (that is, formula c is true).

D5) h is *acceptable* for S at t = Df h is not unacceptable for S at t (that is, formula c is false).

D6) h is *counterbalanced* for S at t = Df Believing h is not epistemically preferable to believing *not-h* for S at t and believing *not-h* is not epistemically preferable to believing h for S at t (that is, formulae b and e are false).

D7) h *ought to be withheld* by S at t = Df h is unacceptable for S at t and *not-h* is unacceptable for S at t (that is, formulae c and d are true).

D8) h is *evident* for S at t = Df For every proposition i, believing h is epistemically preferable to withholding i for S at t.

II

The epistemic concepts just defined pertain to the epistemic status which a single proposition may have for a given subject at a given time. There is also a family of epistemic concepts pertaining to the relations that may hold between two propositions when one of the propositions may be said to confer some epistemic status upon the other. Thus one proposition may be said to *confer evidence* upon another: the one makes the other evident. Or it may confer some lesser epistemic status—reasonability, say, or acceptability, or the status merely of having some presumption in its favor. Or it may confer a negative epistemic status upon the other—that of having no presumption in its favor, or of being gratuitous, or of being unacceptable. Let us call such relations "conferring relations."

We may consider these relations in two ways: in an *absolute* sense as relations holding merely between propositions (or sets of propositions); or in an *applied* sense as relations holding between propositions *for* a particular subject at a particular time. Thus if we take "*e* confers evidence upon *h*" in its absolute sense, we will be concerned with a relation that holds necessarily between the two propositions *e* and *h*, no matter what epistemic status the two propositions may actually have for any subject at any time. But if we take it in its applied sense, saying "*e* confers evidence upon *h* for *S* at *t*," we will be concerned, not only with the relation that holds necessarily between the two propositions, but also with the epistemic status which the propositions happen to have for that particular subject at that particular time.

In order to define these conferring relations we must make use of the concept of *necessity* as well as that of *belief* and those that may be defined in terms of our epistemic primitive. We shall consider only some of these relations in what follows. We begin with the relation that holds between two propositions when the one may be said to make the other evident.

Let us note first that some propositions may be said *deductively*—or *demonstratively*—to make other propositions evident. The absolute sense of this relation may be defined as follows:

D9) *e* deductively confers evidence upon *h* = Df *e* entails *h*, and necessarily, for any subject *S* and any time *t*, if *e* is evident for *S* at *t*, then *h* is evident for *S* at *t*.

We make three comments on this definition: (i) The second clause of the definiens does not follow from the first. There are propositions *e* and *h* which are such that, although *e* entails *h*, it is possible for *e* to be evident for a subject *S* and *h* not to be evident for *S*. This may be the case if it is not evident for *S* that *e* entails *h*. But other propositions *e* and *h* are such that *e* entails *h* and necessarily, for any subject *S*, if *e* is evident for *S*, then *h* is evident for *S*. Presumably "Jones is ill and Smith is away," for example, cannot be evident unless "Smith is away" is also evident. (ii) It is essential that the term "necessarily" appear in the second clause of the definiens; otherwise the definiens would be too broad. We would have to say, for example, that if *e* entailed *h* and if *e* and *h* were evident to no one, then *e* deductively confers evidence upon *h*; or that if *e* entailed *h* and both were evident to one person at the same time and never evident to anyone at any other time, then *e* deuctively confers evidence upon *h*. A similar comment may be made of the definitions that follow. (iii) In the present definition and in those that immediately follow, we will allow ourselves to interpret the variables in the positions of *"e"* and *"h"* in such a way that they will refer, not only to propositions, but also to sets of propositions. When they have the latter interpretation, the following alternative readings are recommended: replace *"e* confers evidence upon *h"* by "the set of propositions *e* confers evidence upon the set of propositions *h"*; *"e* entails *h"* by "the conjunction of the members of *e* entails the conjunction of the members of *h"*; *"e* is evident" by "each of the members of *e* is evident"; *"S* believes that *e* is true" by "each of the members of *e* is such that *S* believes that it is true"; and so on.

D10) *e* deductively confers evidence upon *h* for *S* at *t* = $_{Df}$ *e* is evident for *S* at *t*, and *e* deductively confers evidence upon *h*.

We shall also assume that one proposition, or set of propositions, may *inductively* confer evidence upon another—in other words, that a proposition *e* may confer evidence upon a proposition *h* even though *e* does not entail *h*. Thus we reject the sceptical view according to which there is no reason to believe that the premises of an inductive argument ever confer evidence upon the conclusion. If this view were true, then we would know next to nothing of the world around us.[6]

May we define "*e* inductively confers evidence upon *h*" merely by revising (D9), the definition of "*e* deductively confers evidence upon *h*," and saying that *e* does not entail *h*? In other words, may we say that *e* inductively confers evidence upon *h* provided only (i) *e* does not entail *h* and (ii) necessarily, for any subject *S* and any time *t*, if *e* is evident for *S* at *t* then *h* is evident for *S* at *t*? If we define the relation in this way, then it will be problematic whether the relation ever obtains and therefore we will have conceded the sceptic's point. For if *e* does not entail *h*, then it may well be possible for there to be a man for whom *e* is evident and for whom *h* is not evident, in which case the proposed definiens will be inapplicable. For example, certain things which are evident to you and me inductively confer evidence, for us, upon the proposition that the sun will rise tomorrow. It would be logically possible, however, for there to be a man who has, not only the evidence that you and I have about the solar system, but certain other evidence as well (say, that the solar system will undergo a general cataclysm this evening) which is such as not to make it evident to *him* that the sun will rise tomorrow.

I suggest that the absolute sense of the relation of inductively conferring evidence be defined as follows:

> D11) *e* inductively confers evidence upon *h* = *Df* *e* does not entail *h*; possibly there is an *S* and a *t* such that *e* is evident for *S* at *t* and everything evident for *S* at *t* is entailed by *e* and *h*; and necessarily every such *S* and *t* is such that *h* is evident for *S* at *t*.

6. ". . . in common discourse we readily affirm, that many arguments from causation exceed probability, and may be received as a superior kind of evidence. One would appear ridiculous who would say, that it is only probable that the sun will rise tomorrow, or that all men must die; though it is plain we have no further assurance of these facts than what experience affords us." David Hume, *A Treatise of Human Nature*, ed. L. A. Selby-Bigge (Oxford, 1888), Book I, Part III, Section XI, p. 124.

This definition is consistent with saying both (i) the evidence that you and I have inductively confers evidence upon the proposition that the sun will rise tomorrow and (ii) there may be a man who has the evidence that we have but who, because of certain additional evidence that he has, is one for whom it is not evident that the sun will rise tomorrow. For such a man would not satisfy the terms of our definiens.

How, then, are we to define the applied relation—"*e* inductively confers evidence upon *h* for *S* at *t*"? We will not want our definition to be applicable only to those subjects whose evidence is restricted to what is entailed by *e* and *h*. We will want it to apply to subjects for whom many other things are evident as well. To obtain the desired definition, let us first introduce the more general concept, "*e* confers evidence upon *h*," or "*e* makes *h* evident":

D12) *e* confers evidence upon *h* (*e* makes *h* evident) = Df Either *e* deductively confers evidence upon *h* or *e* inductively confers evidence upon *h*.

And now I propose the following:

D13) *e* inductively confers evidence upon *h* for *S* at *t* = Df *e* is evident for *S* at *t*, *e* inductively confers evidence upon *h*, and, for every *i*, if *i* is evident for *S* at *t*, then the conjunction, *i* and *e*, confers evidence upon *h*.

Let us note that, in countenancing the possibility that one proposition may inductively confer evidence upon another for a given subject, we also countenance the possibility that a proposition may be both evident and false. For there is nothing to guarantee that, if *e* inductively confers evidence upon *h* for *S*, then *h* is true.

We have noted that there are many "conferring relations." Propositions may confer not only evidence upon other propositions, but also reasonability, acceptability, unacceptability, gratuitousness, and so on. But we will consider just one additional conferring relation—that of *confirmation*. Our definition will be similar in an important respect to the definition above (D11) of "*e* inductively confers evidence upon *h*." Let us say:

D14) *e* confirms *h* = *Df* Necessarily, for any subject *S* and any time *t*, if *e* is evident for *S* at *t* and if everything that is evident for *S* at *t* is made evident by *e*, then *h* has some presumption in its favor for *S* at *t*.

It will be recalled that, by (D3) above, the second clause of the definiens is replaceable by "believing *h* is epistemically preferable to believing *not-h* for *S* at *t*."[7]

It may be of interest to note in passing that we are also able to assign one plausible interpretation to *"e* confirms *h* more highly than *i* confirms *j*."* Thus we may define *"h* is of *higher epistemic status* for *S* at *t* than *i* is for *S'* at *t'* "* by saying: "Either *h* is evident for *S* at *t* and *i* is not evident for *S'* at *t'*, or *h* is beyond reasonable doubt for *S* at *t* and *i* is gratuitous for *S'* at *t'*, or *h* is acceptable for *S* at *t* and *i* is unacceptable for *S'* at *t'*, or *h* has some presumption in its favor for *S* at *t* and *i* has no presumption in its favor for *S'* at *t'*." And now we may interpret *"e* confirms *h* more highly than *i* confirms *j"* as saying: "Necessarily, for any subjects *S* and *S'*, if *e* is evident for *S* at *t* and every proposition that is evident for *S* at *t* is entailed by the conjunction, *e* and *h*, and if *i* is evident for *S'* at *t'* and every proposition that is evident for *S'* at *t'* is entailed by *i*, then *h* is of higher epistemic status for *S* at *t* than *j* is for *S'* at *t'*."

The applied concept, *"e* confirms *h* for *S* at *t*,"* may now be defined as follows, in analogy with (D13):

D15) *e* confirms *h* for *S* at *t* = *Df* *e* is evident for *S* at *t*, *e*

7. The first clause may be compared with that of the following informal explication proposed by Carnap: "To say that the hypothesis *h* has the probability *p* (say, 3/5) with respect to the evidence *e*, means that for anyone to whom this evidence but no other relevant knowledge is available, it would be reasonable to believe in *h* to the degree *p* or, more exactly, it would be unreasonable for him to bet on *h* at odds higher than *p*: $(1-p)$." Rudolf Carnap, "Statistical and Inductive Probability," in Edward Madden, ed., *The Structure of Scientific Thought* (Boston, 1960), pp. 269–279; the quotation appears on page 270. Compare Carnap's *Logical Foundations of Probability* (Chicago, 1950), p. 164. In the latter passage Carnap refers to a subject who "knows *e*, say, on the basis of direct observations, and nothing else."

confirms h, and, for every i, if i is evident for S at t, then the conjunction, e and i, confirms h.

Let us now turn to the concept of knowledge.

III

The traditional definition of knowledge may be put as follows:

S knows at t that h is true $=$ $_{Df}$ h is true, S believes at t that h is true, and h is evident for S at t.

In countenancing the possibility that a proposition e may inductively confer evidence upon a proposition h, we also countenance the possibility that e is true and h is false and therefore that there are some propositions that are both evident and false. But Professor Gettier has shown that, if there are propositions that are both evident and false, then the traditional definition of knowledge is inadequate. It is necessary, therefore, to revise the traditional definition. I wish now to suggest that we can revise the traditional definition in terms of the vocabulary that we have introduced here.

What Gettier has shown is that the traditional definition is inadequate to the following situation. (i) There is a set of propositions e such that e inductively confers evidence for S upon a certain false proposition f; (ii) S accepts the false but evident f; (iii) f confers evidence for S upon a true proposition h; and (iv) S accepts h. The traditional definition, in application to this situation, would require us to say that S knows that h is true. But it is clear that, in such a situation, S may not know that h is true.

Gettier cites the following example. (i) There is a set of propositions e such that e inductively confers evidence for Smith upon the false proposition f that Jones owns a Ford. We may suppose that e contains such propositions as these: "Jones has at all times in the past within Smith's memory owned a car, and always a Ford" and "Jones has just offered Smith a ride while driving a Ford."[8] (ii) Smith accepts the false but evident f ("Jones owns a Ford"). (iii) We may assume that f deductively confers evidence upon the disjunctive proposition h that either Jones owns a Ford or Brown is in Barcelona. And we will suppose that, as luck would have it and entirely unsuspected by Smith, Brown *is* in Barcelona. Therefore h ("Either Jones owns a Ford or Brown is in Barcelona") is true. And (iv) Smith, who sees that f, which he believes to be true, entails h, also believes that h is true. Hence the proposition "Either Jones owns a Ford or Brown is in Barcelona" is a proposition which is such that: it is true, Smith believes that it is true, and it is evident for Smith. But our description of the situation does not warrant our saying that Smith knows it to be true.

What has gone wrong? Smith's evidence for h is *defective* in that it confers evidence upon a proposition that is false.[9] To repair the traditional definition of knowledge we must add a qualification to exclude such defective evidence. But how are we to put this qualification? Of the possibilities that first come to mind, some exclude too much and others exclude too little.

8. Some authors, I believe, have been misled in two respects by Gettier's example: (a) He has used "justify" where I have used "confer evidence upon." But "justify" may also be taken to mean the same as the weaker "confer reasonability upon" or even "confer acceptability upon" (not defined here but definable after the manner of D13). The example given would not be counter to the traditional definition of knowledge, if e could be said, only in one of these weaker senses, to justify h; it is essential that e confer evidence upon h. (b) The two propositions which Gettier cites as members of e ("Jones has at all times in the past within Smith's memory owned a car and always a Ford" and "Jones has just offered Smith a ride while driving a Ford") are not themselves sufficient to confer evidence for Smith upon the false proposition f ("Jones owns a Ford"). At the most, they justify f only in the weaker sense of making f reasonable or acceptable. In discussing the example, however, we will imagine that e contains still other propositions and that it does confer evidence upon f for Smith.

9. I borrow this use of "defective" from Ernest Sosa; see his "Propositional Knowledge," *Philosophical Studies*, xx (1969), pp. 33–43.

Shall we say, for example: "If a man knows a proposition h to be true, then *nothing* that confers evidence upon h for him confers evidence upon a false proposition"? This would exclude too much. Consider some proposition k that the Smith of Gettier's example does know to be true and suppose that Smith accepts the conjunction of k and f, where f is the false but evident "Jones owns a Ford." Since the conjunction, k and f, confers evidence upon k for Smith and also upon the false proposition f, the proposed qualification would require us to say that Smith does not know that k is true.

Should we say: "If a man knows a proposition h to be true, then *something* that confers evidence upon h for him is such as *not* to confer evidence upon any false proposition"? This would exclude too little. Suppose that the h of Gettier's example ("Jones owns a Ford or Brown is in Barcelona") does not confer evidence upon any false proposition for Smith. Then there will be something which deductively confers evidence upon h for Smith and which confers evidence upon no false proposition; this something could be h itself as well as the conjunction of h with various other nondefective evident propositions. Hence the proposed qualification would require us to say that the Smith of Gettier's example does know h to be true.

Should we say: "If a man knows a proposition h to be true, then something that *inductively* confers evidence upon h for him is such as to confer evidence upon no false proposition"? This, too, would exclude too little. Consider the disjunction, e or h, where e is the set of propositions that inductively confers evidence upon h for Smith. Like e itself, the disjunction, e or h, inductively confers evidence upon h for Smith. And if it is such as to confer evidence upon no false proposition, then, once again, the proposed qualification would require us to say that Smith knows h is true.

Should we say: "If a man knows a proposition h to be true, then something that inductively confers evidence upon h for him is such that (i) h does not confer evidence upon it for him and (ii) it confers evidence upon no false proposition for him"?

This, too, excludes too little. Suppose Smith accepts the disjunction, "e or (h and p)," where p is any other proposition. If this disjunction confers evidence upon no false proposition, we will still be committed to saying that Smith knows that h is true.[10]

Have we construed "e confers evidence upon h" too broadly? We began by considering a single "h-evidencer"—a single set of propositions e which conferred evidence upon h for S. But we have seen that even our simple example involves many additional h-evidencers. In addition to e there are: h itself; the disjunction "h or e"; the disjunction "(h and p) or e," where p is any proposition; the disjunction "(e and p) or h"; the conjunction "e and k," where k is any other evident proposition; thus also the conjunction "e and f," where f is a false but evident proposition; and such disjunctions as "(e and f) or h" and "(h and p) or (e and k)."

It is clear, I think, that the e of Gettier's example is *central* in a way in which some of Smith's other h-evidencers are not. Of the various possible ways of marking off this centrality, the following seems to me to be the most simple.[11]

> D16) c is a central h-evidencer for S = Df Whatever inductively makes h evident for S is equivalent to a disjunction of mutually consistent propositions one of which implies c.

If, as we will assume, any disjunction of h-evidencers is itself an h-evidencer, then every proposition that has an inductive evidencer will also have a central evidencer—namely, the disjunction of all its evidencers. The e of Gettier's example is thus a central h-

---

10. I am indebted to Professor Gettier for the points made in this paragraph and the one that precedes it.

11. One might define "e is a central h-evidencer for S" by saying "If C is the property of (i) making h evident for S and (ii) being implied by the conjunction of *not-h* with any proposition that makes h evident for S, then e has C and e implies anything that has C." But a definition of knowledge in terms of this sense of central evidencer would involve complications with respect to our knowledge of propositions that are logically true (inasmuch as the negation of such propositions imply every proposition).

evidencer.[12] So, too, is the disjunction "*e* or *h*," as well as the disjunction of all of Smith's *h*-evidencers; though *e*, it may be noted, implies the other central *h*-evidencers.

It is not difficult to see that the other *h*-evidencers on our list are *not* central *h*-evidencers. Consider, for example, "*e* and *f*" where *f* is a false but evident proposition and where "*e* and *f*" inductively makes *h* evident. This will not be a central *h*-evidencer. For there will be some other evident proposition *k* of this sort: "*e* and *k*" inductively makes *h* evident; and "*e* and *k*" is not equivalent to a disjunction of mutually consistent propositions one of which implies "*e* and *f*". (It is, of course, equivalent to a disjunction of mutually *inconsistent* propositions one of which implies "*e* and *f*"—namely, "(*e* and *k* and *f*) or (*e* and *k* and *not-f*).")

What, then, is the peculiar defect of the *h* of our example ("Jones owns a Ford or Brown is in Barcelona")? One of its defects is this: some of its evidencers make evident a falsehood. But as long as any false proposition is evident to Smith, *h* will share this defect with every proposition that is evident to him. Another defect is this: one of *h*'s *central* evidencers—namely, *e*— makes evident a falsehood. But *h* shares this defect with *e* itself —which, presumably, is a proposition Smith knows to be true. For the relation of making evident is transitive; we may assume that *e* has central evidencers; but *e* makes evident the false "Jones owns a Ford"; and therefore *e*'s central evidencers also make evident the false "Jones owns a Ford." What defect does *h* have, then, that *e* does not have?

Though *e*, like *h*, is such that some of its central evidencers make a falsehood evident, *e*, unlike *h*, is equivalent to a conjunction of propositions no one of which is such that *its* central

12. It will be recalled that *e* is comprised of such propositions as these: "Jones has at all times in the past owned a car and always a Ford" and "Jones has just offered Smith a ride while driving a Ford." We have been assuming that there is not another independent set of propositions *e'* which makes *h* evident for Smith—where *e'* might include such propositions as "Jones has just bought a car from the local Ford dealer" and "Reliable and trustworthy authorities affirm that Jones owns a Ford." If there were such an independent set *e'*, then neither *e* nor *e'* would be a central *h*-evidencer, but the disjunction "*e* or *e'*" would be a central *h*-evidencer.

evidencers make a falsehood evident. Thus "Jones has always owned a Ford in the past" does not make evident the false "Jones owns a Ford"; nor does "Jones has just offered Smith a ride while driving a Ford." These propositions (along with the others we are imagining to make up e) are such that collectively they make evident a falsehood but individually they do not make evident a falsehood. We may say, then, that e, unlike h, is "evidentially nondefective" in this sense:

D17) e is evidentially nondefective for S = $_{Df}$ e is evident for S and is equivalent to a conjunction of propositions each of which is such that none of its central evidencers for S makes evident any falsehood.

To be known, then, it is not sufficient that a proposition be true, believed, and evident; it should also be evidentially non-defective.[13] More precisely:

D18) S knows that h is true = $_{Df}$ h is true, S believes that h is true, and h is evidentially nondefective for S.

Given this broad sense of "S knows that h is true," we can readily specify more restricted senses. Thus we could obtain a second sense by stipulating that some of S's central h-evidencers

13. We may note that, if there are any propositions which are evident for S but which are such that nothing inductively makes them evident for S, then these propositions will have no central evidencers and will therefore be evidentially nondefective by this definition. Presumably such propositions are restricted to certain psychological propositions about oneself, to certain propositions which are necessary and a priori, and to whatever such propositions deductively make evident. (In *Theory of Knowledge*, p. 23n, I defined a "basic proposition for S" as a proposition which is evident for S and made evident for S only by what entails it.) What if there is a logical truth h which is such that some proposition e inductively makes h evident for S? If e were itself a logical truth, then all of S's h-evidencers would be central, by our definition, for each would imply e. I suggest, however, that e would be logically contingent; either it would be something like an appeal to authority ("All the experts and reputable texts say that h is true"), or it would contain something like a summary of an induction ("h is of such-and-such a sort, and every proposition of that sort which has been investigated up to now has been shown to be true").

be propositions which he knows, in this first sense, to be true.

If this account is adequate, we may answer Professor Gettier's question, "Is justified true belief knowledge?" by saying: "Yes, provided the justification is nondefective."

IV

What now of the applicability of our various epistemic terms—"evident," "beyond reasonable doubt," "acceptable," and so on? In considering this question, we turn from epistemic logic to epistemology. To answer it, we may attempt to formulate certain epistemic rules or principles—rules or principles describing the conditions under which a proposition may be said to be evident, or to be beyond reasonable doubt, or to be acceptable; and similarly, for our other epistemic terms. In attempting to formulate these rules, we should procede as we do in logic when we formulate rules of inference, or as we do in ethics when we formulate rules telling one the conditions under which a state of affairs may be said to be good, bad, or neutral, or an action may be said to be obligatory, or wrong, or permitted. The procedure is thus essentially Socratic. We begin with certain instances which the rules should countenance and with certain other instances which they should not countenance. And we assume that by reflecting upon these instances and asking ourselves, Socratically, "Just why should our rules countenance cases of the first sort and not countenance cases of the second sort?", we will arrive at certain general criteria.

It is sometimes said that such ethical theories as hedonism are theories telling us what sorts of characteristics are "good-making characteristics" or "better-making characteristics." One could say, analogously, that the attempt to formulate epistemic criteria of the sort described is an attempt to say what sorts of characteristics are "evidence-making characteristics," or "reasonability-making characteristics," or even "epistemically-better-making characteristics."

In the book, *Theory of Knowledge*, I proposed "a sketch of a theory of empirical evidence" and formulated nine such principles. The set of principles was conceded to be incomplete and I noted that "corrections of detail may well be required." As a result of Professor Heidelberger's criticisms, in his article "Chisholm's Epistemic Principles," I now see that the latter observation was true and that the principles I had formulated should be modified in a number of respects.

In what follows, I shall describe briefly certain types of principles or rules which, I believe, are essential to any adequate theory of evidence. The reader who is interested in further details is referred to the original sketch and to Professor Heidelberger's paper. I shall describe eight different types of rule or principle.

1) The first type of principle was summarized in *Theory of Knowledge* as follows: "If there is a 'self-presenting state' such that S is in that state, then it is evident to S that he is in that state" (p. 44). The formula should be thought of as holding for any subject and any time. It should also be thought of as being an abbreviation for a large set of principles that are more specific— more specific with reference to the "self-presenting state" that is involved. Meinong's technical term "self-presenting state" was used to refer to certain thoughts, attitudes, and experiences which were assumed to be such that it is evident to a man that he is thinking such a thought, taking such an attitude, or having such an experience if and only if he *is* thinking such a thought, taking such an attitude, or having such an experience.

Examples of the more specific principles of this first type would be: "Necessarily, for any S and any t, if S believes at t that Socrates is mortal, then it is evident to S at t that he then believes that Socrates is mortal"; "Necessarily, for any S and any t, if S thinks at t that he perceives something that is red, then it is evident to S at t that he then thinks he perceives something that is red." Other principles of this sort would refer to such intentional phenomena as hoping, fearing, wishing, wondering; for example, "Necessarily, for any S and any t, if S wonders at *t* whether the peace will continue, then it is evident to *S* at *t* that he then wonders whether the peace will continue." Still others would refer to certain ways of sensing or being appeared to. Thus there is a possible use of "is appeared to redly" which is such that, if we give the expression that use, then we may say: "Necessarily, for any *S* and any *t*, if *S* is appeared to redly at *t*, then it is evident to *S* that he is then appeared to redly."

2) To introduce the second set of principles, I shall begin with the earlier, inadequate formulation that appears in *Theory of Knowledge:* "If *S* believes that he perceives something to have a certain property *F*, then the proposition that he does perceive something to be *F*, as well as the proposition that there is something that is *F*, is one that is *reasonable* for *S*" (p. 43). The expression "*S* believes that he perceives something to have a certain property *F*" was used in a rather special sense to refer to what is sometimes called a "spontaneous act of perception." The expression "takes," or "perceptually takes," is sometimes used in a similar way. Thus if a man can be said to *take* something to be a dog, in this sense of "take," his act will be entirely spontaneous and not reached as the result of reflection, deliberation, or inference.[14] And if the man is rational and honest, then, in answer to the question, "What is your justification for thinking you know there is a dog here?", he will say that he *perceives* something to be a dog—that he sees, or hears, or smells, or feels there to be a dog. A man can thus take there to be a dog, in the pres-

---

14. In *Perceiving: A Philosophical Study* (Ithaca, New York, 1957), I have discussed "perceptual taking" in more detail; see pp. 75–77. "Taking" is preferable to "believing that one perceives," in the present context, for the latter expression, unlike the former, suggests a higher-order propositional attitude (believing) which has *another* propositional attitude (perceiving) as its object. If a man takes there to be a dog, in our present sense of "take," the object of his attitude is, not another propositional attitude, but simply the being of a dog. "Taking," in this sense, might be said to be related to "perceiving" in the way in which "believing" is related to "knowing." Perceiving (or "veridical perceiving") and unveridical perceiving are both species of the common genus that is here called "taking," or "thinking-that-one-perceives."

ent sense of the term "take," when in fact no dog is there to be taken.

Why not have the simpler rule: "If a man *perceives* there to be a dog then the proposition that a dog is there is one that is reasonable for him"? What this simpler rule states is, of course, true. But to apply it one would need a criterion for deciding when in fact one *does* perceive a dog. Our more complex rule, on the other hand, was intended to provide such a criterion; for the *taking* to which it refers is one of the "self-presenting states" with which the first set of rules is concerned.

The second rule, then, was designed to tell us of certain conditions under which we could say that, for a given subject, a proposition is beyond reasonable doubt. But the rule is much too permissive. For it countenances as being beyond reasonable doubt certain propositions which are hardly worthy of this epistemic status. The point was clearly made by Heidelberger:

> As applied to a particular case, principle (b) tells us that if a man believes that he perceives a certain object to be yellow then the proposition that he does perceive that object to be yellow and the proposition that that object is yellow are reasonable for him. But let us suppose that the following facts are known by that man: there is a yellow light shining on the object, he remembers having perceived a moment ago that the object was white, and at that time there was no colored light shining on the object. Suppose that, in spite of this evidence, he believes that he perceives that the object is yellow. It would not be correct to say that for our man the proposition that the object is yellow is a reasonable one. Merely from the fact that a man believes that he perceives something to have a certain property F, it does not follow, accordingly, that the proposition that that something is F is a reasonable one for him; for, as in our example, he may have other evidence which, when combined with the evidence that he believes that he perceives something to have F, may make the proposition that something is F highly unreasonable. (Op. cit., p. 75)

Our rule was intended to give the senses their due, so to speak, but it gave them far more than they deserve. Clearly some kind of restraint is necessary.

In what sense, then, can we say that taking, or thinking-that-one-perceives, confers reasonability upon the proposition that one does in fact perceive? We could say this: if the only things that were evident to a man were the proposition that he does, say, take something to be yellow, along with whatever propositions this proposition entails, then, for such a man, the proposition that he does in fact perceive something to be yellow could be said to be beyond reasonable doubt. But this fact does not constitute a principle we could apply to any particular case, since there is no one whose evidence is thus restricted. In order to have a principle we can apply, I suggest we say this: the proposition that one perceives something to be yellow is made reasonable provided (i) the man takes, or thinks-he-perceives, something to be yellow and (ii), of the things that are evident to him, none is such that the conjunction of it and the proposition that he *takes* something to be yellow will *fail* to confirm the proposition that he perceives something to be yellow.

Consider again the man to whom Heidelberger refers. He takes something to be yellow—he thinks he perceives something to be yellow. But he also happens to know that the following set of propositions *i* is true: "there is a yellow light shining on the object, he remembers having perceived a moment ago that the object was white, and at that time there was no colored light shining on the object." Although for the man who knows nothing else, taking, or thinking-that-he-perceives, confers reasonability upon the proposition that he does in fact perceive, the present man, as Heidelberger observes, is not one for whom the proposition that he is perceiving something yellow is thus beyond reasonable doubt. And, I would say, the reason that it is not beyond reasonable doubt lies in this fact: the man's independent information *i* is such that the conjunction of *i* and the proposition that he takes something to be yellow does not confirm the proposition that he does in fact perceive anything to be yellow. Thinking-that-one-perceives something to be yellow not only confirms but also makes reasonable the proposition that one does perceive that something is yellow; but thinking-that-one-perceives something to be yellow in conjunction with the proposition *i* referred to above does *not* confirm the proposition that one does perceive something to be yellow.

I suggest, then, that the members of our second set of epistemic principles might be put in the following form:

> Necessarily, for any *S* and any *t*, if (i) *S* at *t* believes himself to perceive something to be *F*, and if (ii) there is no proposition *i* such that *i* is evident to *S* and such that the conjunction of *i* and the proposition that *S* believes himself to perceive something to be *F* does not confirm the proposition that he does then perceive something to be *F*, then the proposition that he does then perceive something to be *F*, as well as the proposition that something is, or was, *F*, is one that is beyond reasonable doubt for *S* at *t*.

The letter "*F*" may be replaced by any predicate which is such that the result of replacing "*F*" by that predicate in "*S* takes something to be *F*," or "*S* thinks-he-perceives something to be *F*," where "takes" and "thinks-he-perceives" have the special use we have attempted to characterize here, is meaningful.

3) A third set of principles may be obtained from the second in the following way: (a) the predicates that can replace "*F*" in our formulation are restricted to those connoting sensible characteristics; and (b) the expression "is beyond reasonable doubt" in the final clause is replaced by "is evident."

Examples of sensible characteristics are: such visual characteristics as being blue, being green, being black; such auditory characteristics as sounding or making a noise; such somesthetic characteristics as being rough, being smooth; those characteristics that were traditionally called "the common sensibles"; and the relations that are connoted by such expressions as "is louder than," "is similar in color to," and "is more fragrant than."[15]

15. See *Theory of Knowledge*, pp. 46–47, for a fuller list.

The third set of principles would tell us, then, that taking something to have a certain sensible characteristic confers, not only reasonability, but also evidence, upon the proposition that one does in fact perceive something to have that characteristic. Is this too permissive? I have argued elsewhere that, if we are not to be sceptics with respect to our perception of the external world, we must say that the spontaneous act of *taking* confers evidence and reasonability.[16] Otherwise, I believe, we will not be able to say of any synthetic proposition about a physical thing that that proposition is evident to anyone.[17]

4) To be able to apply the members of our second and third

16. See *Perceiving: A Philosophical Study,* chap. 6 ("Some Marks of Evidence"), and " 'Appear,' 'Take,' and 'Evident,' " *Journal of Philosophy,* LIII (1956), pp. 722–731, reprinted in Robert Swartz, ed., *Perceiving, Sensing, and Knowing* (Garden City, New York, 1965).

17. Heidelberger proposes what he calls the "traditional empirical" alternative to our third set of principles. This may be suggested by: "the proposition that an object looks rectangular to a man makes evident the proposition that the object is rectangular" (p. 82). I think this principle, too, is sound—provided that "looks rectangular" is taken in that phenomenal or noncomparative sense which is such that, if it has that sense in the sentence "All rectangular things look rectangular under conditions that are optimum for viewing shape," then the sentence is both true and synthetic. But the proposed principle has other possible interpretations under which it would not be satisfactory. Thus it would be inapplicable if "looks rectangular" were taken to mean the same as "looks the way rectangular objects look under conditions such as those that now obtain" or "looks the way I remember rectangular objects to have looked when I have perceived them in the past." And the proposed principle would be less plausible than any of my third set of principles if "looks rectangular" were taken to mean the same as "looks the way I think-I-remember rectangular objects having looked to me when I have thought-I-have-perceived them in the past" (for surely the object of thinking-that-one-remembers-having-thought-that-one-perceived is not *more* worthy of credence than that of thinking-that-one-perceives). And although the proposed principle, when taken in its first sense above, may be an alternative to my third set of principles pertaining to sensible characteristics, it does not provide an alternative to the *second* set of principles pertaining to other types of perceptual taking.

sets of principles, we must also be able to apply principles of still another sort. For the members of the second and third sets of principles each contain a *proviso*. They tell us that taking something to be *F* confers reasonability or evidence upon the proposition that one perceives something to be *F provided that* the following condition holds: there is no evident proposition *i* such that the conjunction of *i* and the proposition that one takes something to be *F fails* to confirm the proposition that one perceives something to be *F*. Hence our fourth set of principles should tell us what types of proposition *i* are such that the conjunction of *i* and the proposition that one takes something to be *F* fails to confirm the proposition that one perceives something to be *F*. How are we to specify such propositions *i*? I shall attempt only a general characterization.

Such propositions *i* would be propositions casting doubt upon the particular testimony of the senses. They could do this in two ways—either "internally" by constituting conflicting testimony, or "externally" by suggesting the possibility of some perceptual malfunction.

The "internal" case presents no problem. Consider a man who thinks-he-sees something to be the only object in his hand and to be round and who, at the same time, thinks-he-feels something to be the only object in his hand and to be rectangular. We may say that each of these takings casts doubt upon the intentional object of the other. The two takings in conjunction are such as to fail to confirm the proposition that there is just one object in his hand and that object is round, and they also fail to confirm the proposition that there is just one object in his hand and that object is rectangular.

What of the "external" case—those evident propositions *i* which suggest the possibility of perceptual malfunction? If it *were* evident to our subject that his senses were not functioning properly, then, of course, there would be an *i* of the sort described. But we have not yet specified any conditions under which such a proposition *i* might be evident to him. Can we describe such a proposition *i* without assuming that our subject has any evidence beyond that so far countenanced by our principles? Heidelberger's criticisms suggest that he might put the problem in the following way: Can we describe such propositions *i* without abandoning the "program of establishing as evident propositions about physical things entirely on the basis of subjective propositions" (p. 76), where "subjective propositions" are those propositions about "self-presenting states" referred to in our first set of principles?

Here we must distinguish at least two different questions. The first question would be: "Suppose we wish to describe conditions under which the proposition that a man is perceiving some object to be *F* is one that is evident or beyond reasonable doubt for him. Can we do this without assuming that some *other* proposition about a physical object is evident to the man?" The answer to *this* question would seem clearly to be affirmative. For our principles say merely that as long as propositions of a certain sort are *not* evident to the man, then, if he takes something to be *F*, it is evident or reasonable to him that something is *F*.

The second question would be: "Consider the situation of a man taking something to be *F* and his *not* being such that it is evident or reasonable to him that he is then perceiving something to be *F*. Can we describe this situation without assuming that some other proposition about a physical thing is evident or reasonable for him?" Here, too, I think the answer is affirmative. Consider a set of believings, takings, and seemings-to-remember of the following sort: the various propositions which are the intentional objects of the members of the set (the propositions that one believes, takes, or seems to remember to be true) are such that, in conjunction, they are consistent and logically *confirm* the proposition that one is *not* perceiving anything to be *F*. Consider this situation: a man takes something to be yellow; he seems to remember having had a sensory disorder causing him to mistake the colors of things; and he believes that the circumstances that now obtain are of the sort that have always misled him in the past. I suggest that the propositions which are the intentional objects of this seeming-to-remember and this believing are such that they logically confirm the proposition that he is not now perceiving anything to be yellow. And these propositions need not themselves be evident in order for the present testimony of the senses to be discredited. They need only be the objects of believing and of seeming-to-remember; and, by our first set of principles, if they are such objects, then it will be evident to the man that he does thus believe or seem-to-remember.

An adequate formulation of our fourth set of principles, then, would tell us what propositions would *confirm* the proposition that one is *not* perceiving anything to be F. And our principles will say that such propositions are of this sort: the proposition *i* asserting that one believes, takes, or seems-to-remember them to be true will be such that the conjunction of *i* and the proposition that one takes something to be F *fails to confirm* the proposition that one perceives something to be F.

We should remind ourselves that our principles are intended only to formulate *sufficient* conditions for the applicability of our epistemic terms. They are not intended to formulate *necessary* conditions. Thus, from the fact that a man takes something to be yellow under conditions where there is no *i* of the sort we have described, we may infer that it is evident to him that he is perceiving something to be yellow. But, from the fact that he takes something to be yellow under conditions where there is such an *i*, we may *not* infer that it is *not* evident to him that he is perceiving something to be yellow.

5) Our fifth set of principles, pertaining to "thinking-that-one-remembers," or "seeming-to-remember," will be analogous to our second set, pertaining to "thinking-that-one-perceives." But where our second set tells us that thinking-that-one-perceives confers *reasonability* upon the proposition that one does perceive, this fifth set will tell us that thinking-that-one-remembers confers *acceptability* upon the proposition that one does remember. I suggest that the members of this fifth set might be put in the following form:

Necessarily, for any S and any t, if (i) S at t believes himself to remember having at a certain time perceived something to be F, and if (ii) there is no proposition i such that i is evident to S and such that the conjunction of i and the proposition that S believes himself to remember having at that time perceived something to be F does not confirm the proposition that he does then remember having perceived something to be F, then the proposition that he does then remember having perceived something at that time to be F, as well as the proposition that he did perceive something at that time to be F and the proposition that something at that time was, or had been, F, is one that is acceptable for S at t.

6) Our sixth set of principles will be analogous to the third. Where the third describes conditions under which thinking-that-one-perceives confers evidence, the sixth will describe conditions under which thinking-that-one-remembers confers reasonability. The sixth may be obtained from the fifth as follows: (a) the predicates that replace "F" in our formulation are restricted to those connoting sensible characteristics; and (b) the expression "is acceptable" in the final clause of our formulation is replaced by "is beyond reasonable doubt." In short, thinking that one remembers having perceived something to have had a certain sensible characteristic confers, not only acceptability, but reasonability upon the proposition that one does in fact remember having perceived something to have had that characteristic.

7) The seventh set of principles would be analogous to the fourth. The fourth set of principles, it will be recalled, tells of certain conditions under which taking something to be F fails to confer evidence or reasonability upon the proposition that one perceives something to be F. The seventh set, analogously, would specify conditions under which thinking-that-one-remembers having perceived something to be F fails to confer reasonability or acceptability upon the proposition that one does remember having perceived something to be F. If it is possible to formulate an adequate set of principles of the fourth type, then, I think, it is also possible to formulate an adequate set of principles of this seventh type.

8) Our eighth set of principles would make use of the notion of *concurrence*, where this notion is defined as follows: any set of propositions that are mutually consistent and such that no one of them entails any other of them is concurrent provided only that each member of the set is confirmed by the conjunction of all the other members of the set. In *Theory of Knowledge*, I proposed the following, somewhat oversimplified example of a set of concurrent propositions: (h) "There is a cat on the roof today"; (i) "There was a cat on the roof yesterday"; (j) "There was a cat on the roof the day before yesterday"; (k) "There was a cat on the roof the day before the day before yesterday"; and (l) "There is a cat on the roof almost every day."[18]

One example, then, of an epistemic principle making use of this concept of concurrence would be the following, which tells us, in effect, that every perceptual proposition belonging to a concurrent set of reasonable propositions is evident:

Necessarily, for any S and any t, if (i) S at t believes himself to perceive something to be F, if (ii) there is no proposition i such that i is evident to S and such that the conjunction of i and the proposition that S believes himself to perceive something to be F does not confirm the proposition that he does then perceive something to be F, and if (iii) the proposition that he does then perceive something to be F is a member of a set of concurrent propositions each of which is beyond reasonable doubt for S at t, then the proposition that he does then perceive something to be F, as well as the proposition that something is, or was F, is one that is evident for S at t.

18. The notion of concurrence is similar to what H. H. Price has called "coherence" and to what C. I. Lewis has called "congruence"; see Price's *Perception* (New York, 1933), p. 183, and Lewis' *An Analysis of Knowledge and Valuation* (La Salle, Ill., 1946), p. 338. Compare also Bertrand Russell, *An Inquiry into Meaning and Truth* (New York, 1940), pp. 201–202, and Roderick Firth, "Coherence, Certainty, and Epistemic Priority," *Journal of Philosophy*, LXI (1964), pp. 545–557.

Any adequate theory of empirical evidence would include canons of inductive logic and doubtless many other epistemic principles as well. But, I am certain, it would also include principles of the sort I have tried to describe.

Max Black
Induction and Experience

I think that it is not only legitimate to appeal to induc-
tive reasoning in defending inductive reasoning, but that
it is indispensable. This is a rather audacious statement
to make, because it looks like defending a vicious circle.
But I believe all procedures of self-clarification, of making
clear to ourselves what it is we have in mind, are in a
way circular. We clarify B through A, and then we turn
around and explain A with the help of B. If a person
were unable to distinguish valid from invalid steps in
inductive reasoning, even in the simplest cases, in other
words, if he were inductively blind, then it would be
hopeless to try to convince him of anything in inductive
logic.*

SAMUEL BUTLER once said that thinking about thinking was like
having an itch—the more you scratch the more you want to
scratch. The same could be said of theorising about theorising,
especially when the theories investigated are the most basic of all
—the very procedures of inference that we employ in providing
rational justification, explanation, and clarification for anything.
But there is no remedy for philosopher's itch. Even at the risk
of lapsing into incoherence and nonsense, a philosopher feels
the urge to thrust against the limits of justification and clarification and to view as problematic the very principles that normally
define what counts as rational.

I shall undertake one such exercise in radical clarification, by
considering certain selected aspects of the relations of inductive
rules to their success in practice. The sorts of questions I want
to raise include the following: Can and should accumulated experience about the use of inductive rules modify our trust in
them? In favorable cases, can the successful employment of induc-

* Rudolf Carnap, "Inductive Logic and Inductive Intuition" in I. Lakatos,
ed., *The Problem of Inductive Logic* (Amsterdam, 1968), p. 264.

tive rules provide rational grounds for increased confidence in the rules? Are we enmeshed in hopeless circularity if we try, in this way, to draw inductive lessons about induction? If not, why not?

Before I plunge into the main discussion, it may be helpful to state informally some of the preconceptions or prejudices with which I approach the subject. I find it natural to think of induction as an institution and, indeed, as a rule-governed one. That is to say, as a system of human activities, involving appropriate concepts, expressed in a distinctive terminology and also involving distinctive rules for the derivation of judgements. The inductive institution commits its participants to labelling certain situations in prescribed ways, to drawing inferences in prescribed fashions, and, notably, to adopting certain cognitive attitudes preparatory to taking appropriate actions. Thus the "institution" has nonlinguistic as well as linguistic aspects. Roughly speaking: inductive rules tell us what to say, how to think, and, within limits, how to act. All of which is intermeshed with higher-level critical activities of appraisal and evaluation.

As to the controversial issue of the inductive institution's overall purpose, it may suffice for now to think of it as intended to generate rational judgement, that is to say, justifiable cognitive commitments concerning the as-yet-not-so-well-known on the basis of the relatively-better-known. In short, to facilitate and legitimize the notorious "inductive leap."

I shall not pause to argue with those who derogate this goal as a self-defeating effort to achieve the impossible. Although the inductive institution plays only a limited part in the vaster enterprise of science, recourse to induction at certain crucial junctures is indispensable, in science as in everyday life. Those who hope to avoid appeal to inductive inference by relying upon the deductive "corroboration" of daring conjectures still let induction in through the back door. If we are to avoid a debilitating skepticism concerning the possibility of any empirical knowledge whatever, we shall have to find a place, however modest, for justifiable inductive inference.

Anyone who thinks of induction as a social instrument designed to further certain enduring human interests in rational conjecture cannot conceive it to be immaculately generated or immutably constituted. To be sure, from within any rule-governed institution, the imperatives of the practice have the force of unquestionable demands. "That is the way the game has to be played!" But a philosopher will always itch to take a look "from the outside," as it were. It would be remarkable indeed if the inductive institution, unlike all others, were in principle immune from external criticism: one would expect it to be responsive to the lessons of practice—knowledge about its degree of success or failure in achieving its proper goals ought surely to be relevant, to make some difference. I believe this to be true, and if true, it must be possible. But showing *how* it is possible is no easy matter.

If you ask a man in the street why we should continue to trust some particular principle of inductive inference, he will almost certainly invoke its past successes. Of course, such a question will seem to the innocent layman odd in the extreme. He will have taken it for granted, for as far back as he can remember, that drawing a sample of black balls from a bag provides *some* good reason for expecting that most of the balls in the bag are black, and the suggestion that there might be some doubt about the soundness of this kind of reasoning will be disconcerting. But inside every "ordinary man" there is a philosopher waiting to emerge: the question about justification, once raised, will seem relevant and in need of a reasoned reply. Once the question is seriously entertained, what could be more natural than to point to past successes, that is, to treat the relevant rule of inference as an instrument that has, on the whole, worked well in the past and therefore deserves our confidence in the future? The only alternative is the unpalatable one of treating the outcome of the employment of inductive rules of inference, both in the past and in the future, as irrelevant. Some philosophers have taken this position, to be sure, but even they, I would suppose, would sooner or later be required to explain how and why inductive procedures can be useful.

An appeal to past successes in defense of an inductive principle, however plausible it may seem, is open, however, to a familiar objection of circularity. In order to fix our ideas, let us consider the following principle:

"When a large sample, drawn at random from some collection of things, shows all the members of the sample to share a certain common property, then other things drawn at random from the same collection will (probably) also have the property in question." Let us call this principle E (for eduction). The deliberate imprecision of the formulation of E need not bother us at this stage of our discussion.

The layman's argument for trusting E can be put in the following form: "E has worked in the past (that is, has usually generated true conclusions from true premises); hence we may expect it to work in the future." To which philosophers, almost unanimously, object by pointing out that there is a missing premise, to the effect that what has worked in the past will continue to work. Now this is itself an inductive principle, or a special case of an inductive principle—roughly speaking, a license to infer from the character of a sample to a corresponding character of the population from which the sample was drawn. Indeed, it looks very much like a special case of E itself, applied to a random sample of inductive inferences. Hence the man in the street is *assuming* that induction "works," when he appeals to past successes: worse still, he seems to be assuming something like the very thing that he is trying to prove, namely that E is trustworhy. So the argument "begs the question," is viciously circular, and the same must be true of every attempt to support induction by appeal to its successes in the past. In Hume's words: "It is impossible, therefore, that any arguments from experience can prove this resemblance of the past to the future; since all these arguments are founded on the supposition of that resemblance."[1] Let us call this "the circularity objection."

1. David Hume, *An Enquiry Concerning Human Understanding,* ed., L. A. Selby-Bigge (Oxford, 1902), Section iv, p. 38.

A principle of inference that generates true conclusions from true premises, in most instances of its use, might be called *reliable*. Now if the circularity objection is well founded, it would seem impossible for us to have any good reasons for thinking any contingent proposition about the external world to be true or even to be more likely true than false. For the proposition that a given rule of inductive inference is reliable, that is that it yields true conclusions from true premises most of the time, is itself a contingent one, expressing some very general truth about the world, about how things behave. If induction "works" on the whole, that is if the principles of inference that we actually use are in the main reliable, that is a matter of fact, not of logic. And the same can be said of those very broad principles, such as Keynes' Principle of Limited Variety, or substitutes for it, whose truth is needed in order for any known system of inductive logic to succeed in conferring nonzero probability upon any contingent proposition.

I am assuming that in the inductive inferences under consideration the conclusion is not entailed by the conjunction of the premises; that is to say, I am assuming that inductive inference is not a species of demonstrative or deductive inference. On this assumption, it seems obvious, at first sight at least, that any claim about the reliability of some principle of inductive inference must be an assertion about matters of fact that might be falsified in some possible world.

Suppose I am playing a game against you in which I present a coin showing heads or tails at my pleasure, while you guess aloud each time what my choice will be: it is clear that I could defeat your prediction each time, no matter how sophisticated your inductive procedures, provided that you announced each prediction in advance of my choice. It is plausible to extend this model to the entire universe and to suppose that a malicious demon, with boundless powers, subject to the constraints only of logical possibility, but not bound by what we call "laws of nature," could similarly arrange to defeat our best inductive efforts. And if being thus constantly frustrated, we began to draw morals from our repeated failures and to modify our procedures accordingly, perhaps by adopting a "counterinductive" policy, the demon could respond to such adjustments, just as successfully as before, provided he still knew our predictions in advance. It seems, therefore, that the world might (in the sense of logical possibility) be so disorderly as to defeat all attempts at inductive inference.

I fear, however, that even this line of argument is not as secure as it might at first appear. It could be argued that, in a world as thoroughly disorderly as the one envisaged, language and thought would be impossible. For built into the vocabulary we use are references to other persons, to material objects and so on, that have implications of inductive regularity and would become unintelligible otherwise. Imagine, if you can, sentient beings attempting to communicate in a situation in which all experience was in Heraclitean flux, and nothing stayed put long enough to be recognized. Clearly enough, in a condition of such chaos and disorder—if indeed the very possibility is conceivable—language and much else would be impossible. It might therefore be argued that the fact that we do have a language and are able to think implies some degree of world order.

Attractive as such a "transcendental" argument may be, it is insufficiently precise for my purpose. I shall therefore adopt the somewhat simple-minded view that assertions about the reliability of inductive principles are straightforwardly contingent assertions of fact.

In any case, I think that a resolute skeptic would not be disarmed by such an argument: Might he not retort that we know at best that we have been able to think and speak *in the past*, and that it remains an open question whether we shall be able to do so in the future? And so we are brought back, again, to the argument from past successes.

Now it would be very remarkable if some contingent propositions, like Keynes' principle, differed from all other contingent propositions in being utterly beyond the reach of empirical support. The truth seems rather to be that if experience does not and cannot support the reliability of any inductive principles, experience cannot provide a basis for rational belief in any contingent empirical principles. The rejection of empirical support for induction leads, as Hume clearly saw, directly to unqualified skepticism about the possibility of knowledge or rational belief about the truth of all empirical propositions. The issue to be discussed is, therefore, of quite fundamental importance.

Hume said, as my earlier quotation illustrates, that no argument from experience could prove the "resemblance of the past to the future," since any such argument must be "founded on the supposition of that resemblance." Let us apply this objection to the layman's argument in defense of the future reliability of the principle I called *E*. (*E* was the principle purporting to justify inference from the sharing of a common property by the members of a randomly drawn sample to the probable possession of that property by further, randomly drawn, members of the population.) The layman's argument runs as follows:

a) *E* has been reliable in a random sample of inferences in the past. *Therefore,*

b) *E* will be reliable in further randomly selected inferences in the future.

Hume's objection, I take it, is that the argument, if this is all there is to it, is a blatant *non sequitur:* the conclusion simply does not follow from the single premise. We ought therefore to treat the layman's argument as an enthymeme, with the missing premise, say:

c) If *E* has been reliable in the past, then it will be reliable in the future.

Now, with the addition of (c), the argument becomes valid, being an obvious instance of *modus ponens.* If you do not care for the specific form of the unstated additional premise, I can imagine Hume saying, you will have to choose another one at least as strong, that is to say, another premise which, in conjunction with the original premise (a), will entail (b). For anything weaker than this will leave the reconstructed argument invalid.

But (c), the weakest premise that will serve, claims that reliability of E in the past is sufficient to ensure reliability in the future. And how could we know this to be true—or, for that matter, know it to be even probable? Either you have no reason to assert it, except the desire to present a valid rather than an invalid argument—or else you must take it as a special case of the correctness of arguing from a shared character of the members of a sample to the presence of that character in further members drawn at random. In other words, your only good reason for asserting the extra conditional premise must be your commitment to the principle E, which is just what was in dispute. It sounds like a knock-down objection.

I have taken Hume to be treating the "layman's argument" as intended to be demonstrative, so that in questioning the possibility of a "proof," he was attacking the possibility of offering an argument in support of E's reliability that would employ premises known to be true, or at least probably true, and would also be valid.

The first answer to this attack is that the layman's argument is—or, at least, ought to be taken as being—nondemonstrative. But in nondemonstrative or inductive inference, as I conceive it, we have to be clear from the outset that the canons of demonstrative inference are inapplicable. By definition, a nondemonstrative inference, whether correct or not, is one whose conclusion is not a demonstrative consequence of the premises. Thus, the accusation of lack of validity or, failing that, of "circularity" is, strictly speaking, beside the point. To reject such arguments on the score of vicious circularity and to complain that an inductive inference is not "valid" is like complaining that a hammer is not much use as a walking stick or that butter is not a good glue: it is to fall into the old trap of confusing nondemonstrative inference with demonstrative inference, and so into illicitly judging the correctness of inductive inference by canons appropriate only to deductive inference. (Incidentally, if the argument from experience were circular, as alleged, it would certainly be valid in the deductive sense, no matter what other faults it had. But a nondemonstrative inference does not aspire to be valid.)

However, I fear that this first retort to Hume, though important and sound, may seem unsatisfactory, and for good reason. A sympathetic critic might grant, at least proleptically, that inductive inference, if there is such a thing, is entitled to have its own standards of correctness, distinct from demonstrative validity, and yet remain dissatisfied with the "layman's argument." Even if it is clear that we are not seeking a proof of the conclusion, by means of a valid argument, is there not a gap between the single premise and its conclusion? Should it not, perhaps, be treated as an inductive enthymeme, lacking a further premise, logically weaker than the one previously supplied, but still lacking it, for all that?

In order to answer this, we must distinguish between inductive arguments that are genuinely incomplete, and others that only seem so, in virtue of the attraction of the deductive model of inference. If I argue: "that man has turned pale, so he is probably angry," I might, reasonably enough, be challenged to explain why I treat the premise as a reason for the truth of the conclusion, even though I am understood to be arguing nondemonstratively. I might then offer the extra premise, "men who turn pale in that way are usually angry," which fleshes out the original argument, by offering further relevant information, while still leaving it nondemonstrative. But if I am asked, with regard to the expanded argument, why I treat the conjunction of the two premises as a reason for the conclusion, it would be inappropriate to look for a further substantive premise. The conclusion already follows, with probability; the expanded version is already an inductive, nondemonstrative, argument of the correct form, whose premises support the conclusion in accordance with a correct rule of inference. Any further objection must be to the type of argument used, rather than to the completeness of the argument itself—and that is a different matter. To counter such radical criticism by offering further premises would be to behave as foolishly as Achilles in his celebrated encounter with the tortoise. Once Achilles had provided an argument having the form of *modus ponens*, or some other valid form of deductive argument, Achilles ought to have stopped adding premises and should have refused to go on. Once we have elaborated a non-demonstrative argument, originally using some unstated premise, into a form in which it has become an instance of a correct form of inductive argument, we too are entitled to stop. The chain of reasons, as we have been reminded, must end somewhere.

The situation with regard to the layman's argument is that no further premises are needed: the argument *as it stands*, and without benefit of additional premises, exemplifies a correct form of inductive argument. Only the form of argument used is either the same as that of the principle *E* that is in question, or is suspiciously like it. One might therefore justifiably look upon the whole argument as a sort of hocus-pocus. To be sure, it may be innocent of invalidity, given that we are aiming at something other than validity. The conclusion is no part of the argument's premises, so the accusation of formal circularity is out of place. But is there not a more subtle circularity involved in *using* the very principle whose credentials are in question to establish its own credentials? Is this not dangerously like taking a man's own word for his credibility?

Let me state in a summary way what I take Hume's attack to have established. I think he showed, at the very least, that the notion of a demonstrative *proof* of the reliability of induction is a chimera. And I think we can go further than this. The idea that the layman's argument, or anything resembling it in relying upon past successes with inductive methods, could refute wholesale skepticism about inductive inference seems equally chimerical. You cannot persuade anybody by argument who distrusts and rejects all argument; and you cannot persuade somebody who distrusts and rejects all inductive argument by means of an inductive argument. But in this respect inductive argument is in no case worse than deductive argument. There are limits to what can be shown by means of deductive argument concerning the validity of deductive argument; and it would be unreasonable to demand more of inductive argument.

There remains, however, more to be said about the layman's argument, if it is treated, not as a wholesale attempt to refute skeptical objections about induction but rather as an attempt to show that past experience is relevant to the assessment and, sometimes, to the refinement and the improvement of inductive procedures. I shall try to show in what follows that this kind of appeal to experience is possible, and that the progressive character of inductive procedures depends upon it.

Inductive inferences, like deductive ones, can be subject to certain kinds of paralysing weaknesses, having some analogy at least to deductive "circularity." I shall try to show that some appeals to experience in support of the reliability of inductive rules are free from such defects and really do succeed in raising the antecedent credibility of their conclusions.

For the sake of having a definite and relatively precise illustration, I shall use an old and much-discussed illustration.

Consider the following rule of inductive inference:

> R: To argue from *Most instances of* A's *examined under a wide variety of conditions have been* B to (probably) *The next* A *to be encountered will be* B.

And also consider the following "self-supporting argument" in its defense:

> A: In most instances of the use of R with true premises, examined in a wide variety of conditions, R has been successful.
>
> *Hence (probably)*
>
> In the next instance to be encountered of the use of R in an argument with a true premise, R will be successful.

Here, it looks as if the rule governing the argument A is the very same rule that is to be supported by the conclusion. The danger of some kind of circularity, perhaps not that of explicitly assuming the conclusion, seems patent.

In order to forestall possible misunderstanding, I shall now interpolate some explanations about how the illustrative argument A is to be understood.

a) By "success," I mean the generation of a true conclusion from true premises; a rule that is successful most of the time I call "reliable." Clearly, there can be degrees of reliability, ranging from 0 to 1.

b) By "the next instance" of the rule's application, I mean much the same as "another instance selected at random." The difference in meaning between these two expressions is unimportant for what follows.

c) I find it appropriate to require that the conclusion of A (and of other nondemonstrative arguments) be taken to be "detached." This is to say, I am treating the illustrative argument A as offered in support of the unqualified assertion of R's success in another instance; the argument in question does not terminate in a conclusion *about* the probability of further success of the rule. (The function of the word "probably" in the illative link—"Hence [probably]"—is explained below.)

Is it proper to conceive of the conclusions of inductive inferences as "detached," in the way I have proposed? This issue remains controversial. In favor of this view, it can be urged that only in this way can we regard inductive inferences as providing conclusions that make testable assertions about the world. By contrast, the canonical form of an inductive conclusion in Carnap's reconstruction of inductive logic is $c(h, e) = n$, whose analyticity is a consequence of the choice of a particular confirmation function, c, for a given language. Now, if the only acceptable conclusions of inductive inference had to be conceived as analytic, it would be hard to see how they could constitute genuine information about the world. Of course, Carnap and his followers rely upon a rather elaborate account of how analytical inductive conclusions can be connected, via personal utilities, with bets and perhaps other actions under uncertainty. In company with other critics, I find this way of connecting up confirmations or—what comes to the same thing, probability-assertions—with actions unsatisfactory. It is, for instance, very hard to make sense of rational bets on the truth of generalizations or abstract scientific theories.

Even if one rejects Carnap's view of the matter, but still insists that a proper conclusion should contain a reference to probability in the form, say, of *prob* $(h/e) = n$, one is still faced with the awkward problem of verification and applicability to test-situations. For the probability assertion is compatible with the falsity of h, no less than with its truth. What, then is being said about the world?

The strongest objection to the detachment view that I know is the contention, forcibly argued by Professor C. G. Hempel and others, that it leads to so-called "inductive inconsistencies." On certain evidence, E_1, I might be led to "detach" the conclusion h; but, given certain other evidence, E_2, I might also have to "detach" the contradictory conclusion, *not-h*. Thus, it is said, I might well find myself in the embarrassing position of having to assert on good grounds both h and its contradictory.

One answer to this might take the form of a *tu quoque*. For somebody like Hempel, who hopes to establish the connection between probability assertions and rational actions via bets based upon calculations of expected utilities, the situation envisaged, in which different bodies of evidence point in opposite directions, might well be held to lead to "inductively inconsistent" *actions*. If E_1 provides me with good reasons, given my scale of utilities, for betting on the truth of h, while E_2 provides me with equally good reasons for betting on *not-h*, what am I to do? Thus the problem of "inductive inconsistencies" might be viewed as a special case of the important but unsolved problem of "total evidence." However, this reply does not go to the heart of the matter.

Lurking behind Hempel's bogy of "inductive inconsistencies" there may be an unacceptably rigid conception of the nature of rational assertion. He seems to suppose that if, on evidence E_1, I am justified in asserting h, then I am committed to reiterating that same assertion—standing by it, as it were—no matter what other facts come to light. But if I subsequently come into possession of evidence E_2, that, taken alone, would have led me to assert the contrary conclusion, not-h, I am certainly entitled to review the situation. The rational decision would be to strike h from my stock of accepted assertions (though without impugning the correctness of the previous judgement made on the partial evidence E_1) and to suspend judgement as between h and not-h, pending some way to amalgamate all the evidence now at hand. As another writer has well said: "It seems plain that a man can be completely certain of some proposition, yet, later, as he learns new evidence, come to doubt it. This is a veritable mark of rationality."[2]

I would add that the whole issue becomes clearer if we take account, in a way now to be explained, of the "index of credibility" which, in sophisticated formulations, should be taken as attached to the conclusions of inductive inference.

d) In presenting the illustrative argument A above, I attached the qualifying word *"probably"* to the sign of illation, *"Hence,"* in order to emphasize, as already explained, that I wished no reference to probability to be part of the content of the argument's conclusion. Of course, the qualification, *"probably,"* might also have been attached to the conclusion. But then it ought to be regarded, as already suggested, as a parenthetical modifier, attached to the whole embedded sentence to which it is attached. Its role, in such parenthetical use, I take to be that of facilitating the expression of what might be called a *qualified assertion.*

It is common, in ordinary speech, to qualify an assertion by inserting some parenthetical expression that warns the hearer, in a fashion whose utility is obvious, about the speaker's degree of confidence in making the assertion in question. Consider such assertions as *"With some hesitation,* I say the fine weather *will*

2. Ian Hacking, *The Logic of Statistical Inference* (Cambridge, 1965), p. 223.

continue" or *"To the best of my knowledge,* his name is Smith" or
"I have good reason to believe that opium is beneficial to the nerves."
Each of these remarks, if made with appropriate intonation and
in an appropriate setting, commits the speaker to a categorical
assertion: he claims, as the case may be, that the fine weather will
continue, that the name of the person in question *is* Smith, that
opium *is* beneficial to the nerves. Yet at the same time the speaker
supplies his hearer with a useful signal concerning his own confidence in the strength of his reasons for making the assertion
in question. (I neglect any more specific information that may be
transmitted concerning the nature of the backing evidence.) I
construe the parenthetic clause as a side remark, not part of the
main assertion but a cautionary comment about it. (Similarly, a
scientific instrument may have attached to it a cautionary statement about its reliability that is no part of the instrument's
readings but usefully warns the user as to the degree of confidence he should attach to any such readings.)

I wish to interpret the occurrence of "probably" in my illustrative case of a self-supporting argument in just this way. The
presence of the word "probably," whether attached to the sign
of illation or to the conclusion, warns a reader that a nondemonstrative argument is in question. It alerts him therefore to the
absence of entailment between the premise and the conclusion;
and prepares him to treat the assertion actually made in the conclusion as provisional and therefore modifiable in the light of
further evidence, as previously explained. But although this *index
of credibility,* as I propose to call it, does "qualify" the assertion,
in the fashion outlined, it leaves the assertion as a straightforward truth-claim: you cannot more or less assert something—
assertion is a hit-or-miss affair. And however much the speaker
qualifies his assertion, he is still *making* the assertion and will
be shown to have been in error if it proves to be false. Consider a limiting case such as the remark "I just have a hunch,
nothing more, (and my hunches are notoriously unreliable) that
inflation *will* cease this year." If this weak-kneed remark is made
with a characteristically assertive intonation for the embedded

sentence "Inflation *will* cease this year," the speaker is committed to the truth of that assertion and will have to admit that he was wrong if the facts fail to support him. (Of course, his having indicated the weakness of his grounds for making the assertion functions retroactively as an excuse for his mistake. To qualify an assertion is, as it were, to take the sting out of possible defeat by conceding fallibility in advance.)

"Probably" is, of course, a very crude index of credibility. In ordinary life we distinguish between "barely probable," "more probable than not," "very probable," "almost certain," and so on. It is therefore natural to envisage sophisticated ways of presenting inductive arguments in which the simple qualification "probably" might be replaced, at least in special contexts, by a graded index of credibility. In favorable cases, indeed, it seems plausible to locate the appropriate index of credibility within a numerical interval or even to estimate its numerical value. When a standard symbolism is used, such a quantified index of credibility might be imagined preceding an assertion, within a square bracket. In such a formulation, the premises of an inductive inference would have their own indices of credibility and the canonical form of our original argument would look like this:

$$A': \quad [n_1] \ P$$
$$Hence \ (probably)$$
$$[n_2] \ K$$

where 'P' is supposed to be replaced by the original premise supplied in A, 'K' is supposed to be replaced by the original conclusion, and 'n_1' and 'n_2' are supposed to be replaced by definite numbers marking the respective indices of credibility of the premise and the conclusion.

From here on, I shall assume that the argument before us is expressed in this sophisticated and more precise form. Thus, the argument form A, or its more precise variant A', should be conceived as a schema. A "self-supporting" defense of an inductive rule should be regarded as an argument intended to raise the antecedent credibility of its conclusion.

Let us turn now to a detailed examination of the reasons that can be urged for or against the supposed circularity of the argument A'. It would be helpful if we could begin with some explicit understanding of what is intended by the imputation, always pejorative, that a given argument is "circular." But it is surprisingly difficult to produce a suitable definition. The most blatant case of "vicious circularity," in which the conclusion appears explicitly as a premise, offers no trouble—though even here it is worth making once again the obvious point that such an argument is at least valid. We need a more general formula to cover not only such cases of unabashed circularity, but also others not of this type, that are equally objectionable. For instance: any argument to the conclusion K, having as one of its premises the conjunction $K \cdot L$, obviously needs to be rejected as having no probative force, although the conclusion is not identical with any of the premises. But what would be a general formula to cover all the intended cases?

I have been unable to find a satisfactory answer to this question in the literature. Indeed, the only serious discussion of the point that I know is in W. E. Johnson's unsatisfactory distinction between what he calls "epistemic" and "constitutive" conditions of inference.

The task of finding a satisfactory analysis of the notion of "vicious circularity" is perhaps not insoluble. I propose, however, to bypass it here. What matters for our present inquiry is whether a particular form of inductive argument, looking suspiciously "circular," whatever that may mean, can serve the proper ends of induction. This approach has the advantage of highlighting the reasons for regarding "circularity" as reprehensible. (The label we apply to this, or to an allied defect, is unimportant; what we need to know is the character of the imputed fault and the reasons why it is objectionable.) Let us call an inference, whether deductive or inductive in character, *effective* when it fulfills the purpose for which such an inference is designed: I propose now to examine the conditions of effectiveness for both types of inference.

Let us begin with the conditions for effectiveness of deductive inference. The purpose of a deductive inference may usually be regarded as that of raising the antecedent credibility of the conclusion: in the most favorable case, a proposition whose truth was antecedently doubtful is rendered certain by being deduced from premises all of which are certain; in the more general case, a proposition whose initial credibility was, say, p has its credibility raised to q, where q is greater than p, by being deduced from premises whose joint credibility is q. (I must ignore in this paper some relevant and pressing questions about what "credibility" means and how it is to be established. I am, at any rate, thinking of "credibility" as relative to available evidence, but not otherwise "subjective.")

Given this conception, we can now state the *objective conditions* for a deductive inference having the amalgamated premise P, and the conclusion K, as follows:

i) K must follow from P by means of a *valid* rule of inference (that is $P \cdot \sim K$ must be a contradiction).

ii) The credibility of P must be higher than the antecedent credibility of K. (From which it follows that if condition (i) is fulfilled, the credibility of K will be raised by the inference in question.)

These conditions, I may add, seem to me both necessary and sufficient. But these objective conditions must now be supplemented by some *subjective conditions* for effectiveness. That these are relevant can easily be seen by considering that a deductive inference might satisfy both the foregoing conditions and so be in some sense an acceptable inference, without yet providing a thinker with any good reasons for increased confidence in the conclusion. Suppose the reasoner does not think the rule of inference he is using to be valid; then the inference in question cannot be made in good faith and does not provide him with acceptable reasons for increased confidence in the conclusion—even if the principle of inference is in fact valid.

As a first try, I suggest the following conditions for subjective effectiveness:

iii) The reasoner must *think* that the rule of inference he employs is valid.

iv) The reasoner must *think* that the credibility of the amalgamated premise is higher than the antecedent credibility of the conclusion.

Roughly speaking, then, the reasoner must believe that the objective conditions obtain.

It might perhaps be objected that the last two conditions are necessary but not sufficient. For it may be that the reasoner, though believing the argument to be objectively effective, has no good reasons for his belief. We might therefore try to strengthen our schedule of conditions for subjective effectiveness by demanding that the reasoner's beliefs shall themselves be thought by him to have sufficient grounds (where grounds are appropriate), and this enlarged set of conditions might in turn be strengthened by insisting that those grounds (the reasoner's reasons for holding the inference to be objectively effective) shall themselves be good grounds. And so on. Clearly we have here a gamut of sets of conditions of variable severity, ranging from simple belief in objective effectiveness, through grounded belief, to relatively well-grounded belief, with possible complications introduced by considerations concerning the strength and quality of the reasons in question.

I shall ignore these complications here and will satisfy myself with the formula: A deductive inference is *fully effective* if it is objectively effective (raises the antecedent credibility of the conclusion by the use of a valid rule of inference) and is held to be so, on sufficient grounds (a deliberately vague phrase) by somebody presenting or accepting the inference.

If we now try to apply a similar analysis to the case of inductive inference, the only change needed is the substitution of reliability for validity in our conditions. For what makes an inductive rule of inference good, I suggest, is its capacity to generate true conclusions from true premises most of the time—that is what I have been calling its reliability. This being granted, the effectiveness of the inductive inference, in its "subjective" aspects, will depend upon whether the reasoner is entitled, as before, to think, and with good reason, that he is using a reliable rule to raise antecedent credibility. I shall therefore say that an inductive inference is fully effective if (1) the rule of inference used does yield true conclusions most of the time and does raise the antecedent credibility of the conclusion, and if (2) a given reasoner thinks and has sufficient grounds for thinking that it does both of these things. It looks sufficiently obvious that no fully effective argument can be objectionably "circular."

Let us now see whether an argument of the form A' is "fully effective" in the sense explained. I will take the relevant conditions seriatim.

a) *Does A' use a reliable rule of inference?* This, as I have said before, is a question of fact, as to whether a certain procedure does in practice yield a certain desired result most of the time: it is, therefore, in principle, no different from a question such as: Does boiling eggs usually result in making them hard? I believe there can be no serious doubt about the answer: I take it to be *true* (and I hope none of my readers will think otherwise) that we do get better results by using inductive rules than we would by using so-called "counterinductive" rules. I mean, of course, that the relevant inductive rule not only has worked in the past, but also will work in the future. Here, a skeptic's qualms are irrelevant, since the reliability of the inferential rule is not a premise of the argument. In any case, as I have already explained, the argument is not directed against wholesale inductive skepticism. The only question, for the moment, is whether the rule R is in fact reliable, and to this the answer seems to me plainly, yes.

b) *Does A' confer a higher credibility upon its conclusion than it antecedently had?* In other words, once we have the evidence stated in the amalgamated premise of A', do we have more reason to expect that R will be successful upon a new occasion than we had before considering the argument? Here again, I cannot see how one can possibly deny it. The evidence is certainly relevant, if we are interested in R's further application: it would be contrary to everything we know to insist that the status of the conclusion (its credibility) is unaffected by the new evidence.

c) *Do we have sufficient reason to think R antecedently reliable?* This can hardly be answered offhand, given the vagueness of the expression "sufficient reason," and the doubts that may perhaps be raised as to when we are entitled to say we have good or sufficient reasons. An opponent might say that if the question were pressed, objectionable circularity would reappear upon considering the alleged reasons at our disposal. I wish only to insist—and this is really my main point—that there is nothing about the form of inference A' to make it impossible, for logical reasons, for us not only to think R reliable, but even to have good reasons, of varying degrees of force, for so thinking. Nor does such well-grounded belief, if it should be at our disposal, render the inference superfluous because "ineffective." For what such well-grounded belief assures us, and all that it needs to assure us, is that R works more often than not. The point of the given inference, however, is to *increase* the credibility of R's successful application in a new instance. Now even if our confidence in R is justified, it is not superfluous to strengthen that confidence for its application in a given instance.

d) *Do we have sufficient reason to think that argument A' will raise the credibility of its conclusion?* That is to say, if the rule R is indeed reliable, are we justified in *thinking* that its application to the presented evidence would make the conclusion more credible than it was before? I am inclined to say that we know this on a priori grounds, and that the granted reliability of the rule will guarantee (deductively!) that the presence of the new evidence will increase the credibility of the conclusion. For consider what is really at stake. We are supposed to think that we have a rule R of such a character that it usually associates a true conclusion with true premises; we are also supposed to think that we have premises that are true, leading by an application of the rule to the conclusion K; given all this, the question is whether we are justified in attributing to K a higher credibility than it would otherwise have had, that is, in claiming that we have *better reason* for asserting K than would otherwise have been the case. The affirmative answer seems to me to be required by our conception of "good reason" (and the associated notions that figure in this line of thought). That anybody fully understanding what is meant by credibility, reliability, good reason, and so forth should refuse to count such a derivation of K as strengthening the grounds in its favor would seem to me to show an insufficient grasp of the relevant concepts. Not to treat K as having its credibility strengthened would be like seeming to reject the application of *modus ponens*. That is a sign, not of inductive blindness, as Carnap implies in the epigraph of this essay, but rather of a more fundamental failure to have mastered the use of certain procedures of reasoning to which we are committed by our language. (Could this have been what Carnap meant?)

On the whole, then, I conclude that there is nothing about the form of argument A, its critics notwithstanding, to impugn its effectiveness. Indeed, I hope to have made it at least plausible that argument A could be fully effective. A fortiori, then, it cannot suffer from any kind of objectionable circularity that would render its use pointless.

There may be something radically wrong with the line of thought I have been presenting; if so, I shall be glad to be corrected. My experience with critics of the "self-supporting" position has been that it leaves even the most sympathetic uncomfortable: even if no specific flaw can be found, they can't help thinking that something must be wrong—the ghost of vicious circularity still haunts the topic. It may therefore be helpful if I refer briefly in conclusion to the objections raised by the most formidable of my critics.

Professor Peter Achinstein, in two powerful and illuminating papers,[3] agrees that the "self-supporting" argument I have been considering is innocent of deductive circularity, and he agrees that, taken as an inductive argument, it contains no reprehensible overt circularity. It does, however, embody a more subtle yet fatal circularity. For in order to have a right to use the rule R in the second-order argument, we have to "assume" that R is reliable. But 'R is reliable' logically implies 'R is successful most of the time' (that is, usually leads from true premises to a true conclusion) which in turn logically implies 'R will probably be successful in the next (or in a random) instance of its use'— which was the very thing that the second-order argument was supposed to establish. Thus in order to argue to that conclusion, we must "assume" something that entails it, namely that the rule is reliable.

If Achinstein were right, let us notice, the contingent evidence about past successes adduced in the first premise of the "self-supporting" argument would be quite irrelevant, because in trying to argue from such evidence we are already committed to more than we are trying to prove. By the same token, no amount of discouraging report about past failures of the rule could have any tendency to impugn that rule's reliability; no amount of unsatisfactory experience with the rule could provide any reason for diminished confidence in the rule. I find this very hard to accept.

Achinstein's objection suffers from an 'all or nothing' attitude to the self-supporting argument, and from failure to consider whether the argument might not have the differential function of strengthening the rule's credibility, rather than "establishing" it. He is right in urging that if we had *no* antecedent reason to use R and to trust it, no inductive argument from past successes could give us a reason to regard R as reliable and hence likely to work

3. Peter Achinstein, "The Circularity of a Self-Supporting Inductive Argument," *Analysis*, xxii (1961–62), pp. 138–141, and "Circularity and Induction," *Analysis*, xxiii (1962–63), pp. 123–127.

in another instance. So used, the argument would indeed be defective. But if we already have some reason to trust R, appeal to past successes may give us better reason to trust it, and evidence of past failures ought to weaken our confidence in the rule. The situation seems to me basically no different from the use of any self-applicable instrument as a check upon its own reliability. If I consult the *Encyclopaedia Britannica* to see what it says about itself, I am, no doubt, "assuming" in something like Achinstein's sense, that the *Encyclopaedia* is generally accurate. Were I to find some article in the *Encyclopaedia* itself accusing the *Encyclopaedia* of gross unreliability, that would be evidence that I could not afford to neglect. By the same token, the absence of such self-depreciating comment is some evidence, however slender, in favor of the assumption of general reliability. Our confidence in inductive rules admits of gradation and can be adjusted in the light of experience. Nothing that Achinstein has urged leads me to believe that there is some fallacy behind this contention.

I will end with a more striking type of objection, presented by Achinstein and others. It takes the form of arguing that my "defense" would "prove" too much: we are offered allegedly "counterinductive" self-supporting arguments which might, it is urged, be used with just as much plausibility (that is to say, quite wrongly!) to support themselves. For instance, the "counterinductive rule" that authorises a transition from the presence of a character in the members of a sample to the *absence* of that character in another member drawn at random could, it is urged, be used to argue from the failure of this rule in the past to its success in the next instance of its use.

I have replied, in the past, that such a "counterinductive" rule would be incoherent in the sense of leading to contradictory conclusions when the "second-order" argument in its defense is invoked. We therefore have a reason for rejecting it which does not arise in the case of the conventional "inductive" rules.

There seems to me, however, a more fundamental reason for

being suspicious about referring to such allegedly "counter-inductive" rules. If we try to imagine a set of people using the term "probably" (and other words belonging to the practice of nondemonstrative inference) in a way which would be consonant with adherence to "counterinductive" rules, we should have to imagine them, also, rejecting the very paradigms that control our own uses of "probably." For example: if a handful of marbles drawn from a bag were all black, the counterinductionists would have to regard that as a clear case of the probability of another ball's being black being diminished. In short they would have built into their practice a convention that distrusted experience.

Now it seems to be very doubtful whether we should be justified in saying that such people would be using "probably" in the same sense as we do. It will hardly do to say that they are inveterate addicts of the gambler's fallacy who simply persist in making mistakes: that would be like saying that people who got addition sums wrong all the time and *were quite satisfied* to do so really meant just what we do by addition—but suffered, merely, from inveterate inability to apply the term correctly. If the wrong sum satisfies them, they cannot mean what we mean by addition—chess played for the sake of losing is not chess but some other game. For such reasons as these, I do not think that the counterexamples of self-supporting arguments for "counter-inductive" rules are much to the point.

My contention could be put in this way: there is an a priori aspect to the rules governing inductive inference and the prac-tices that are demanded of those properly using those rules: given our present language and the system of concepts that it embodies, we are logically unable to imagine wholesale deviations from them. (We are unable to imagine in full detail what a "counterinductive" world would be like.) But this does not mean that we have to be dogmatic: the constitutive rules of the induc-tive institution allow for considerable play in the differential judgements we make concerning inductive conclusions, the reli-ability of rules, and so on. Now it is the purpose of appeal to past experience to supply just such a basis of rational grounds for reinforcing or, within modest limits, for modifying the inductive institution and its components. Appeal to past experience can, however, be only gradualist and revisionist (to use political language): for revolutions in our modes of thought we must look elsewhere.